I0813326

# JAMES

*The Hodder Bible Commentary*

Edited by Lee Gatiss

# JAMES

DANIEL K. ENG

The Hodder Bible Commentary
Series Editor: Lee Gatiss

First published in Great Britain in 2025 by Hodder Faith
An imprint of John Murray Press

1



A CIP catalogue record for this title is available from the British Library

Hardback ISBN 978 1 399 82178 0
ebook ISBN 978 1 529 30242 4

Typeset in Bembo Std and Utopia by Palimpsest Book Production Ltd, Falkirk, Stirlingshire

Printed and bound in Great Britain by Clays Ltd, Elcograf S.p.A.

John Murray Press policy is to use papers that are natural, renewable and recyclable products and made from wood grown in sustainable forests. The logging and manufacturing processes are expected to conform to the environmental regulations of the country of origin.

Carmelite House
50 Victoria Embankment
London EC4Y 0DZ

www.hodderfaith.com
www.hodderbiblecommentary.com

John Murray Press, part of Hodder & Stoughton Limited
An Hachette UK company

The authorised representative in the EEA is Hachette Ireland,
8 Castlecourt Centre, Dublin 15, D15 XTP3, Ireland
(email: info@hbgi.ie)

To my parents, Bunyan and Mamie Eng,
who modeled to me a love for the Scriptures and the church

# *Contents*


Series Preface xi
Consultant Editors xiii
Acknowledgments xv
Abbreviations xvii

Introduction 1
1. *Genre* 2
2. *Author* 3
3. *Date* 5
4. *Themes and distinctives* 6
5. *Structure* 9

1 The Introductory Prologue (James 1) 11
1. *The cohesiveness of James 1* 11
2. *James 1:12 as a thesis statement* 13

2 Prologue 1: Trials, Wisdom and the Lowly (James 1:1–12) 17
1. *Salutation · James 1:1* 18
2. *Trials lead to maturity · James 1:2–4* 20
3. *Single-mindedly asking God for wisdom · James 1:5–8* 25
4. *The great reversal · James 1:9–11* 28
5. *The approved will receive the crown of life · James 1:12* 31

3 Prologue 2: Temptation, Being Quick to Hear and Slow to Anger (James 1:13–27) 35
1. *Temptation is not from God · James 1:13–18* 36
2. *Quick to hear, slow to speak, slow to anger · James 1:19–25* 40
3. *Religion accepted by God · James 1:26–7* 45

4 Structure of James 2 49

5 Eschewing Favouritism, Obeying the Law (James 2:1–13) 51
1. *Thesis statement · James 2:1* 52
2. *Do not favour the rich · James 2:2–4* 53
3. *God favours the poor and opposes the rich · James 2:5–7* 58
4. *One must obey the whole law · James 2:8–13* 62

6 Faith and Deeds (James 2:14–26) 67
1. *Thesis statement · James 2:14* 68
2. *Hypothetical scenario: a needy brother or sister · James 2:15–17* 70
3. *Imaginary debate · James 2:18–26* 71

Excursus: Paul and James on Faith, Deeds and Justification 79

7 Taming the Tongue (James 3:1–12) 85
1. *Opening command: not many should become teachers · James 3:1a* 86
2. *Two reasons to avoid becoming teachers · James 3:1b–2* 87
3. *The power of the tongue · James 3:3–6* 90
4. *The difficulty of keeping the tongue in check · James 3:7–8* 93
5. *Using the tongue singly to bless, not curse · James 3:9–12* 95

8 Display Wisdom from Above (James 3:13–18) 99
1. *Show your wisdom by your good deeds · James 3:13* 101
2. *Warning against demonic wisdom · James 3:14–16* 102
3. *Description and results of heavenly wisdom · James 3:17–18* 106

9 Submit to God (James 4:1–12) 111
1. *Pursuing selfish desires causes strife · James 4:1–3* 113
2. *Being an enemy of God and its remedy · James 4:4–10* 121
3. *Summarising transition: slander and judgment · James 4:11–12* 139

10 Apostrophe (James 4:13–5:6) 145
1. *Apostrophe A: arrogant merchants · James 4:13–17* 146
2. *Apostrophe B: wicked rich · James 5:1–6* 151

11 Persevere Patiently Until Judgment (James 5:7–11) 161
1. *Patient until the end · James 5:7–10* 162
2. *Persevere until the end · James 5:11* 166

12 Final Exhortations (James 5:12–20) 171
1. *No need for oaths · James 5:12* 172
2. *Exhortations to prayer · James 5:13–15* 175
3. *Prayer for sin · James 5:16–18* 181
4. *Restoring a wanderer · James 5:19–20* 185

# Series Preface

*The unfolding of your words gives light*
(Psalm 119:130)

The Hodder Bible Commentary aims to proclaim afresh in our generation the unchanging and unerring word of God, for the glory of God and the good of his people. This fifty-volume commentary on the whole Bible seeks to provide the contemporary church with fresh and readable expositions of Scripture which are doctrinally sensitive and globally aware, accessible for all adult readers but particularly useful to those who preach, teach and lead Bible studies in churches and small groups.

Building on the success of Hodder's NIV Proclamation Bible, we have assembled as contributors a remarkable team of men and women from around the world. Alongside a diverse panel of trusted Consultant Editors, they have a tremendous variety of denominational backgrounds and ministries. Each has great experience in unfolding the gospel of Jesus Christ and all are united in our aim of faithfully expounding the Bible in a way that takes account of the original text, biblical theology, the history of interpretation and the needs of the contemporary global church.

These volumes are serious expositions – not overly technical, scholarly works of reference but not simply sermons either. As well as carefully unpacking what the Bible says, they are sensitive to how it has been used in doctrinal discussions over the centuries and in our own day, though not dominated by such concerns at the expense of the text's own agenda. They also try to speak not only into a white, middle-class, Western context (for example), as some might, but to be aware of ways in which other cultures hear and need to hear what the Spirit is saying to the churches.

As you tuck into his word, with the help of this book, may the glorious Father 'give you the Spirit of wisdom and revelation, so that you may know him better' (Ephesians 1:17).

Lee Gatiss, Series Editor

## *Consultant Editors*

The Series Editor would like to thank the following Consultant Editors for their contributions to the Hodder Bible Commentary:

Shady Anis (*Egypt*)
Kirsten Birkett (*UK*)
Felipe Chamy (*Chile*)
Ben Cooper (*UK*)
Mervyn Eloff (*South Africa*)
Keri Folmar (*Dubai*)
Kerry Gatiss (*UK*)
Kara Hartley (*Australia*)
Julian Hardyman (*Madagascar*)
Stephen Fagbemi (*Nigeria*)
Rosanne Jones (*Japan*)
Henry Jansma (*USA*)
Samuel Lago (*USA*)
Andis Miezitis (*Latvia*)
Adrian Reynolds (*UK*)
Peter Ryan (*Australia*)
Sookgoo Shin (*South Korea*)
Myrto Theocharous (*Greece*)

# *Acknowledgements*

I am grateful to Lee Gatiss, the Series Editor of the Hodder Bible Commentary, and to Hodder & Stoughton for the opportunity to write this commentary on James. Most of my work in the epistle of James has been more academic, so the opportunity to reconsider the letter to serve the church has been edifying to me.

I also thank the Executive Leadership Team and the Board of Trustees at Western Seminary for granting me a sabbatical leave to complete this project. I express my gratitude to the welcoming staff and faculty at Southeastern Baptist Theological Seminary, where I wrote much of this commentary as a Visiting Scholar.

I acknowledge those who read previous drafts and gave valuable feedback. These include Ben Cooper, Johnny Chan, Octo Chow, Adam Christian, Tracy Fabel, Clark Fobes, Christian Gonzalez, Nicholas Hsieh, Jay Lee, KC Liu, R. Todd Moussallem, Matt Ng, Phillip Powers, Abigail Prejean, Adrian Tijerina, Taylor Turkington and Nathan Wong.

Finally, I want to thank my wife, Sanjung, and our daughters Joanna, Josie, and Jessica. Packing up and relocating to North Carolina for a few months took a great deal of energy and patience. Throughout the process, they kept me encouraged while reminding me of my priorities. Yes, Dad is done writing this book.

# *Abbreviations*

| | |
|---|---|
| BDAG | *A Greek-English Lexicon of the New Testament and Other Early Christian Literature*, eds. Walter Bauer, Frederick W. Danker, William F. Arndt and F. Wilbur Gingrich (3rd edition; Chicago: University of Chicago, 2000) |
| LSJ | Henry George Liddell and Robert Scott, *A Greek-English Lexicon: With a Revised Supplement*, ed. Sir Henry Stuart Jones and Roderick McKenzie (Oxford: Clarendon, 1996). |
| LXX | Septuagint (Greek) Text of the Old Testament |

# *Introduction*

'Why are we being treated this way?'

'Is God displeased with us?'

'What hope do we have?'

Life was difficult for Jews outside their ancestral homeland. They were scattered among the nations, in unfamiliar places. The Temple – the centre for their heritage and faith – was far away. In their new homes they were disadvantaged, without access to many goods and services. On top of that, they had trouble. They were being excluded, discriminated against and exploited.

The plight of these Jews led to particular temptations. Their disadvantaged status made them wonder if God was truly good. They were drawn to seek public esteem for themselves or to give special treatment to high-ranking figures. They wanted to hold on to the little wealth they had, rather than be generous to others in their midst. They battled anger and jealousy, even quarrelling and lashing out against one another.

James, the brother of Jesus, wrote a letter to the communities of Jewish Christians. As the leader of the church in Jerusalem, he needed no introduction. In the letter, he addressed their fears, insecurities and temptations. Amid their difficulties, he assured them of their heavenly Father's compassion. He encouraged them that their trials had a good purpose. He gave them confidence that God would penalise their oppressors and make things right in the end.

For followers of Jesus in any era, the epistle of James is a letter of hope. James encourages his readers to endure through their trials in adherence to Christ. The hope of James is not based in this life, but in the afterlife. James constantly writes about end-time judgment. The expectation of the judge is a warning to the unrepentant, but a message of hope for those who persevere.

## 1. *Genre*

James has traditionally been grouped with the *catholic* or *general* epistles. Scholars have given the name 'catholic' to a group of anywhere between six and nine New Testament documents, with disagreement on whether to include John's epistles and Revelation. Nevertheless, James is always included within this designation.

The letter's designation as catholic does not refer to the Roman Catholic Church, but to the letter's recipients. A catholic epistle's audience is said to be general, or nonspecific. However, one could argue that the designation of the recipients, 'the twelve tribes scattered among the nations' (James 1:1) is still specific. Nonetheless, there is no indication of a particular location for the hearers. Ultimately, it is best to see the term *catholic epistles* not as a label of genre, but as a proper name, referring to a specific collection of New Testament letters.[1]

While some reject the notion that James is an epistle,[2] the document shows multiple points of affinity with ancient letters.

1 Darian R. Lockett, *Letters for the Church: Reading James, 1–2 Peter, 1–3 John, and Jude as Canon* (Downers Grove: IVP Academic, 2021), 4.

2 See Martin Dibelius, *James*, trans. Michael A. Williams, (Eleventh edition; Philadelphia: Fortress Press, 1976), 1–3; S. R. Llewelyn, 'The Prescript of James', *Novum Testamentum* 39 (1997): 385–93.

Like other Greek letters which lack situational immediacy, James displays an opening formula with a blessing, thanksgiving and key terms that are repeated later in the document.[3]

Possibly the most compelling evidence that James is an epistle is its conclusion. The end of James contains multiple elements that are typically found in other ancient Greek letters. These include the phrase 'above all' (James 5:12) and content about oaths, health and prayer.[4]

There are a great many commands, or exhortatory content, found in James. But this content does not disqualify this document from being an epistle. After all, exhortation is found in every New Testament epistle. With its opening and closing content demonstrating an affinity with ancient letters, this commentary will treat James as it is framed: as an ancient letter.

## 2. *Author*

The author refers to himself as 'James', with no qualifications regarding his home town or lineage. James was a common name during that time; the fact that this one needs no introduction suggests that he was a prominent James.

At least five men named James are mentioned in the New Testament: (a) James the son of Alphaeus (Matthew 10:3),

---

3 Ancient Greek letters often had a double opening with repeated terms, like James displays. See Fred O. Francis, 'The Form and Function of the Opening and Closing Paragraphs of James and I John', *Zeitschrift für die neutestamentliche Wissenschaft und die Kunde der älteren Kirche* 61 (1970): 110–24. Also, James's opening previews terms and concepts found later in the epistle. More remarkable are terms introduced in James 1 that are rare in the New Testament but repeated later, such as 'double-minded' (1:8), 'doer' (1:22, 23, 25) and 'rein' (1:26).

4 For more about these epistolary elements, see Daniel K. Eng, *Eschatological Approval: The Structure and Unifying Motif of James* (Sheffield: Sheffield Phoenix Press, 2022), 45.

(b) James the father of Judas (not Iscariot, see Acts 1:13), (c) James the son of Mary and Clopas (John 19:25; Mark 15:40),[5] (d) James the son of Zebedee, the brother of John (Matthew 4:21), and (e) James the brother of Jesus, the son of Mary (Mark 6:3; Jude 1). The first three men are not well known enough to have a letter attributed to them that was authoritative to Christians.[6] The fourth one, the brother of John, was martyred in the year AD 44 (or before, see Acts 12:2), which is probably too early for him to be the author of this letter.[7]

Ultimately, there is no compelling evidence that overturns the witness of the early church that this letter was written by James, the brother of Jesus. The church historian Eusebius wrote about this James, called the 'Just' from the time of the Lord.[8] James had an important role in the early church. He was the figure who took an authoritative speaking role at the Jerusalem Council in Acts 15:13–21. The apostle Paul singled him out as a witness to Christ's resurrection (1 Corinthians 15:7) and called him an 'apostle' and a 'pillar' (Galatians 1:19; 2:9).

The epistle of James uses the same opening format as the letter from James to the Gentile believers in Acts 15:23. They both feature the default letter-opening formula of sender-recipient-greeting, and they are the only New Testament letters with the classic word for 'Greetings' (1:1).[9]

---

5 According to Douglas J. Moo, *The Letter of James*, (Second edition; Grand Rapids: Eerdmans, 2021), 11, Jerome first identified these two Marys as the same person. See also Scot McKnight, *The Letter of James* (Grand Rapids: Eerdmans, 2011), 13.

6 Moo, *The Letter of James*, 14–15.

7 Dan G. McCartney, *James* (Grand Rapids: Baker Academic, 2009), 9.

8 *Ecclesiastical History*, 2.23. Eusebius of Caesarea, *Ecclesiastical History, Books 1–5*, trans. Roy Joseph Deferrari (Washington, DC: Catholic University of America Press, 1953), 125.

9 It is found in non-biblical letters. See McCartney, *James*, 40.

## *3. Date*

The letter of James has been dated as early as AD mid-40s and as late as the fourth century.[10] Intimately tied to the question of dating is the identity of the author; some consider the letter to be written by someone else in the name of James. But the arguments for the epistle to have a different author, such as the high register of Greek or the perceived lack of Christian or Jewish distinctiveness, are based on cultural assumptions and speculation. These objections can be countered straightforwardly.[11] Ultimately, with James's probable authorship, we can assign a date for the letter before his death in the year AD 62.

We can deduce an even more specific time frame by examining the epistle's contents. Because of the common language between the documents, some suspect that James is responding to the letters of Paul, especially Roman and Galatians. However, James's argument would be a poor representation of Paul (see the commentary's excursus on Paul and James); the true James would not have misunderstood Paul this badly.[12] We are compelled, then, to place James before Paul's written works.

The letter's content also makes no mention of the break between the church and Judaism, nor does it discuss the mission to Gentiles. With the omission of references to the controversies over circumcision, Sabbath observation and dietary regulations, we can justifiably have the letter of James pre-date the Jerusalem Council (the year AD 48),[13] which would fit before Paul's letters.

10 For a detailed treatment of all the views, see Dale C. Allison Jr, *James: A Critical and Exegetical Commentary* (New York: T&T Clark, 2013), 4–34.

11 See, for example, Craig L. Blomberg and Mariam J. Kamell, *James* (Grand Rapids: Zondervan, 2008), 33–5.

12 McCartney, *James*, 54.

13 So William C. Varner, *James: A Commentary on the Greek Text* (Lexington, KY: Fontes, 2017), 13.

A date between AD mid-40s and AD 48 would make James the earliest New Testament document. It would pre-date the final forms of the Gospel accounts, thus also making it the earliest written attestation of the sayings of Jesus.

## 4. *Themes and distinctives*

The epistle of James has many commands in quick succession. It contains the highest concentration of imperatives in the New Testament, and they are distributed throughout the letter rather than in one section. These commands often occur with explanations and development.[14] The practical nature of James makes it straightforward for the modern reader to teach and preach from.

James has a penchant for pithy, timeless sayings, which often makes it resemble Jewish wisdom literature (for example, 1:12; 2:13; 3:18; 4:17). In particular, the letter shows connections with Proverbs, with at least one quotation (4:6, citing Proverbs 3:34) and other probable allusions (such as Proverbs 2:3–6 in James 1:5 or Proverbs 27:1 in James 4:14).[15]

A repeated motif in James is the concept of *judgment*. Words and concepts related to judgment, judges and courts are spread throughout the epistle (1:6; 2:4, 6, 12–13; 3:1, 17; 4:11–12; 5:9, 12).[16] Consistently, when these terms are used for God, they are esteemed and affirmed. For example, James 4:12 states, 'There is only one Lawgiver and Judge'. However, when the terms are used for humans, the actions are condemned. For example, James 2:4 states, 'Have you not discriminated among yourselves and become judges with evil thoughts?' The cumulative message of

---

14 See the chart in Varner, *James*, 22.

15 McCartney, *James*, 45.

16 These terms derive from the word family of *krisis* (judgment) and *krinō* (to judge).

all this repeated content about judgment is this: There is only one legitimate judge, and he is the Lord.

The epistle contains a great deal of eschatological content. James is keenly concerned about the end times, particularly end-time judgment. He describes a great reversal between those of high status and those of low status (1:9–11; 2:5; 4:6, 10; 5:1–4). James is concerned about the looming judgment (2:12–13; 3:1; 4:12; 5:9, 12). He displays a concern that his hearers will be approved in this judgment and receive a reward (1:12; 2:14; 5:7–11) and not an unfavourable outcome (1:13–15; 2:9–13; 3:10–12; 5:12, 20).

James repeatedly frames his exhortations as a choice between two alternatives. These dichotomies are consistent with the 'Two Ways' motif found in Jewish wisdom literature. Dichotomies include the lowly vs the rich (1:9–11), the results of life vs death (1:13–15), the rich vs poor (2:2–7), blessing vs cursing (3:11–12), wisdom that is earthly vs wisdom from above (3:14–18), and friendship with the world vs friendship with God (4:4). Through this pattern of binary choices, James urges his hearers to choose the better one. In other words, the repeated motif is, 'Be like this and not like that.' Like the Deuteronomic choice to choose good rather than evil and life rather than death (Deuteronomy 30:15–20), James urges his hearers to choose the way that leads to a favourable eschatological judgment.

James's exhortations are largely lived out in the community. With his repeated familial language ('my brothers and sisters'), James demonstrates a collectivistic mindset. Piety, or *religion*, is demonstrated by how one treats the less fortunate (1:27). Having saving faith in James 2:14–17 is lived out through providing for the needs of a brother or sister. On the other hand, James condemns selfishness, jealousy and quarrelling, calling them demonic and 'friendship with the world' (3:14–16; 4:4). He urges his hearers to use their tongues for blessing others who are made in God's image (3:9–12). He affirms the making of peace (3:17–18) and reminds the hearers of the law's call to love their neighbours (2:8; see also 4:12). James even ends the epistle with calls to pray for one another and to bring back those who wander (5:16–20).[17]

James contains more connections with the sayings of Jesus than any other New Testament document outside the Gospels.[18] Most frequently, the allusions to Jesus's sayings come from the Sermon on the Mount (Matthew 5–7) and the Sermon on the Plain (Luke 6:20–49). James writes that God gives good gifts (1:17; see Matthew 7:11; Luke 11:13), demands adherence to the whole law (2:10; see Matthew 5:19) and calls for singular loyalty (4:4; see Matthew 6:24).[19] The clearest allusion occurs in James 5:12, when James writes, 'Do not swear – not by heaven or by earth or by anything else. All you need to say is a simple "Yes" or "No"' (see Matthew 5:34–7).

James shows connections to the other catholic epistles, including themes like human suffering as tests of faith, faith embodied by works, and steadfast obedience leading to eternal life.[20] There is a particular affinity between James and 1 Peter. Both address their audiences as *diaspora* (see the commentary at 1:1), demonstrate a concern for Christian suffering and allude to Proverbs 3:34 and Isaiah 40:6–8.[21]

---

17 I discuss collectivistic culture in James in Daniel K. Eng, 'East Asian and Asian American Reflections on James', *Journal for Baptist Theology and Ministry* 19, no. 2 (2022): 247–8.

18 Patrick J. Hartin, *A Spirituality of Perfection: Faith in Action in the Letter of James* (Collegeville, MN: Liturgical Press, 1999), 2.

19 Peter Davids lists thirty-six probable allusions to sayings in Matthew, Mark and Luke. Twenty-eight are from the Sermon on the Mount/Plain. See Peter H. Davids, *The Epistle of James* (Grand Rapids: Eerdmans, 1982), 48.

20 For an examination of the consistencies across the catholic epistles, see Darian R. Lockett, *Letters from the Pillar Apostles: The Formation of the Catholic Epistles as a Canonical Collection* (Eugene, OR: Pickwick, 2017), 199.

21 McCartney, *James*, 52–3. Also, James 1:2–4 (see the commentary below) and 1 Peter 1:6–7 have multiple connections.

James contains many connections to the Old Testament: from concepts and quotations to even its very words. For example, there are strong parallels to Jewish thinking in the epistle's content on the tongue, humility and wealth. Quotations from the Old Testament include Genesis 15:6 (James 2:23) and Proverbs 3:34 (James 4:6). These quotations often come from the Greek translation of the Old Testament, also called the Septuagint (LXX). There are only thirteen Greek words in James that do not occur in the LXX.[22]

## *5. Structure*

The letter of James displays evidence of how the author is organising his content. As we will discuss in the commentary, James employs the use of *inclusio*, a literary device that uses repeated words to bracket the intervening content into a unit of thought. These bracketed units contain themes that run through the content, indicated by the repeated words at the beginning and end. As we will discuss, there are three significant instances of *inclusio* found in James, which help to frame the intervening content:

1:2–4 to 1:12 and 1:12 to 1:25
1:12 to 5:11
2:12–13 to 4:11–12

The first usage of *inclusio* is a double usage, and it shapes the opening chapter as the introductory prologue of the letter. The brackets point to the key saying in James 1:12, which is the thesis

22 Ben Witherington III, *Letters and Homilies for Jewish Christians: A Socio-Rhetorical Commentary on Hebrews, James and Jude* (Downers Grove: IVP Academic, 2007), 388.

statement of the letter. We will discuss the nature and function of James 1 in the commentary.

Key elements of the thesis statement are also repeated in 5:11. This signals that the main body of James ends at 5:11, and that the intervening material shows the value of persevering in faithfulness with the end times in view.

Finally, the key repeated elements in 2:12–13 and 4:11–12 include the law and divine judgment. These brackets signal that the intervening content urges the hearers to live in adherence to the law in both speech and deeds. They will be judged when the end comes.

In view of the usage of *inclusio*, the structure of James can be viewed like a fish skeleton, with the head of the fish as the prologue and the tail as the reprise of the thesis statement. We will discuss this structure as we proceed through the commentary.[23]

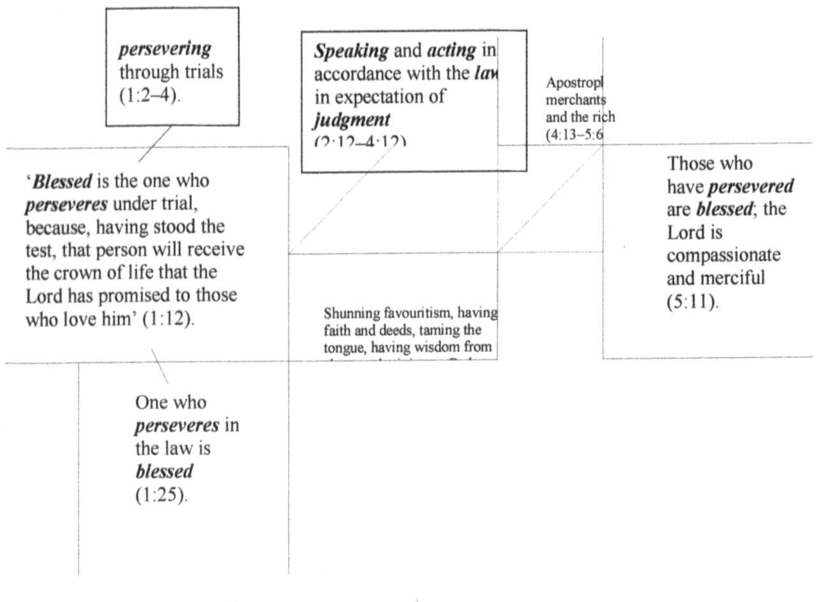


23 Eng, *Eschatological Approval*, 73, 185–6.

# ERRATUM

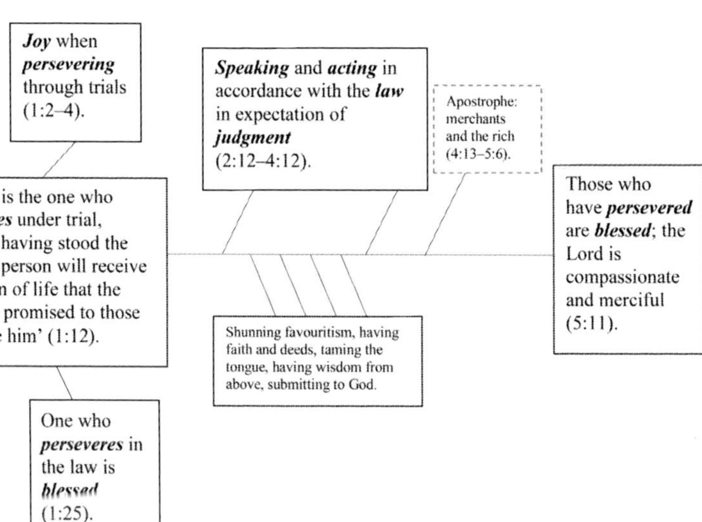


Page 10, *The Hodder Bible Commentary: James*

# I

# The Introductory Prologue

## JAMES 1

Chapter 1 of James serves as a prologue to the letter, introducing the main themes that will run through the document. After discussing the structure of the opening chapter, I will introduce how James 1:12 serves as a thesis statement, and will then provide exposition for its subsections, highlighting how they present concepts that will recur in the rest of the epistle.

### 1. *The cohesiveness of James 1*

While a common view states that James has no continuity of thought, studies in recent decades have challenged this notion.[1] James's opening chapter shows evidence of a cohesive unit. The opening follows ancient Greek letter conventions: the identification of its author and recipients, followed by a greeting. The final content of James 1 (1:26–7) offers a transition into the rest of the letter. The intervening content, James 1:2–25, introduces the letter's major topics. With multiple previews of the letter, the opening of James is like a constellation of stars – individual subunits that can be seen in relationship to one another.

The opening salutation in James 1:1 ends with greetings (*chairein*), which connects to the word 'joy' (*charan*) in 1:2. The

1 For the issues regarding the structure of James, see Alicia J. Batten, *What Are They Saying about the Letter of James?* (Mahwah, NJ: Paulist Press, 2009), 9–16.

exhortation of 1:2–4, as we will discuss below, is a chain-saying that ends with the concept of 'lacking'. The next subsection, 1:5–8, ties to the previous section through the term 'lacks'.[2] Also, the concept of wisdom as necessary to being 'mature and complete' (verse 4) ties 1:5–8 with the previous subsection. Next, James 1:9–11 contrasts the condemnation of the double-minded (1:8) and the favourable assessment of the 'believers in humble circumstances' (1:9).[3]

James 1:12 fits into the opening as a transitional statement. First, it connects to 1:2–3 through the common concepts of trial, test, perseverance and the end-time 'high position' in 1:9.[4] Second, James 1:12 connects with the content proceeding after it. The noun 'trial' *(peirasmon)* in 1:12 is a cognate of the terms for 'tempt' (*peirazō*) in 1:13. An easily overlooked connection occurs between James 1:12 and 1:25, which share the concepts of blessing and perseverance. Thus, James 1:12 serves as an overlapping transition, akin to a fulcrum on a seesaw. As we will see, this shows evidence for an opening formula with repeated elements, as James 1:12 ends the previous section and starts the next. We will discuss the function of 1:12 below.

James 1:13–18 develops the concepts of God as the source of good gifts and not temptation, held together by the imagery of birthing.[5] Next, the content starting at James 1:19 connects to 1:13–18 through several elements, including 'word' (1:18, 21, 22,

---

2 For how catchwords form ties in James, see Daniel K. Eng, 'The Role of Semitic Catchwords in Interpreting the Epistle of James', *Tyndale Bulletin* 70 (2019): 245–67.

3 They are also tied together by the continuative conjunction, *de*.

4 See Luke Timothy Johnson, *The Letter of James: A New Translation with Introduction and Commentary* (New Haven: Yale University Press, 2008), 189–90.

5 Also see Steven E. Runge, *Discourse Grammar of the Greek New Testament: A Practical Introduction for Teaching and Exegesis* (Peabody, MA: Hendrickson, 2010), 111–12.

23) and being deceived (1:16, 22, 26).[6] In 1:19, James's three-part exhortation is expanded by the following sections: being quick to listen (1:22–5), slow to speak (1:26) and slow to anger (1:20–21). The two statements of 'religion' in 1:26–7 connect to previous content through the concepts of being deceived (see 1:16, 22) and having God as the Father (1:17).[7]

## *2. James 1:12 as a thesis statement*

James 1:12 fits best as a standalone statement that serves as an overlapping transition. This saying is the thesis, or summary statement, not just for the opening of James, but also for the entire epistle: 'Blessed is the one who perseveres under trial because, having stood the test, that person will receive the crown of life that the Lord has promised to those who love him.' Set between the salutation (1:1) and transitionary statements (1:26–7), the prologue of James is contained in 1:2–25. As discussed above, James 1:12 has notable connections with both the beginning and end of this content:

| **1:2–4** | **1:12** | **1:25** |
|---|---|---|
| [joy] | blessed | blessed |
| trial | trial | |
| perseverance | perseveres | continues |
| testing | test | |

6 Also, the continuative conjunction *de* and the term translated 'every' or 'all' (*pas*, 1:17, 19, 21).

7 For the cohesive ties in James 1, see Eng, *Eschatological Approval*, 46–59.

| **1:2–4** | **1:12** | **1:25** |
|---|---|---|
| finish its work | | perfect . . . doing |
| mature and complete | will receive the crown of life | |

The connections between the beginning, middle and end of the prologue form a double *inclusio*: the framing of a unit of text using repeated terms in its opening and closing. The content of 1:2–4 and 1:25 point to the fulcrum of this double *inclusio*: James 1:12.

James 1:12 also has connections the end of the epistle's body at 5:11. There, the terms describing blessing and perseverance are repeated. Thus, James displays a grand *inclusio* between the fulcrum saying in 1:12 and the closing content in 5:11, framing the content in between.

| **1:2–4** | **1:12** | **1:25** | **5:11** |
|---|---|---|---|
| [joy] | blessed | | blessed |
| trial | trial | | |
| perseverance | perseveres | continues | persevered, perseverance |

James 1:12, with its connections to 1:2–4, 1:25 and 5:11, serves as a key saying that previews the main message the epistle. As the epistle unfolds, we will see that James urges his hearers to choose the better of two options with each exhortation. As discussed above, the concept of *judgment* is dispersed throughout the epistle, with God being the rightful judge in the end. Throughout the letter, James conveys that, if his hearers choose the better of two

options, they can look forward to a favourable judgment in the end. James 1:12 sums up the epistle's message: 'Blessed is the one who perseveres under trial because, having stood the test, that person will receive the crown of life that the Lord has promised to those who love him.'

## 2

# Prologue 1: Trials, Wisdom and the Lowly

## JAMES 1:1–12

James 1 serves as a prologue that contains words and concepts that will be developed later in the epistle. There is ample support for the opening of ancient Greek letters serving this function. For example, epistles attributed to Paul, after the salutation, typically have content that previews the main topics of the epistle.[1] Also, there exists support that ancient Greek letters repeat the introductory material, creating a twofold introduction like James does in 1:2–4 and 1:12.[2]

In the commentary that follows, I will explain how each subsection of the introductory prologue presents topics that will recur later. For the modern expositor, the prologue can be delineated as two large teaching sections: (a) 1:1–12 and (b) 1:13–27. Alternatively, James 1 can be taught as one unit, with the subdivisions as outlined below.

**1** James, a servant of God and of the Lord Jesus Christ,

To the twelve tribes scattered among the nations:

Greetings.

*Trials and temptations*

**2** Consider it pure joy, my brothers

1 For example, Romans 1:13; Philemon 7–14; Philippians 1:12–18. See Jeffrey A. D. Weima, *Paul* the Ancient Letter Writer: An Introduction to Epistolary Analysis (Grand Rapids: Baker Academic, 2016), 59.

2 For example, Josephus *Antiquities of the Jews*, 8:50–54; 1 Maccabees 10:25–45. For a detailed discussion, see Francis, 'Form and Function', 110–26.

and sisters,[a] whenever you face trials of many kinds, **3** because you know that the testing of your faith produces perseverance. **4** Let perseverance finish its work so that you may be mature and complete, not lacking anything. **5** If any of you lacks wisdom, you should ask God, who gives generously to all without finding fault, and it will be given to you. **6** But when you ask, you must believe and not doubt, because the one who doubts is like a wave of the sea, blown and tossed by the wind. **7** That person should not expect to receive anything from the Lord. **8** Such a person is double-minded and unstable in all they do.

**9** Believers in humble circumstances ought to take pride in their high position. **10** But the rich should take pride in their humiliation – since they will pass away like a wild flower. **11** For the sun rises with scorching heat and withers the plant; its blossom falls and its beauty is destroyed. In the same way, the rich will fade away even while they go about their business.

**12** Blessed is the one who perseveres under trial because, having stood the test, that person will receive the crown of life that the Lord has promised to those who love him.

**a** 2 The Greek word for *brothers and sisters* (*adelphoi*) refers here to believers, both men and women, as part of God's family; also in verses 16 and 19; and in 2:1, 5, 14; 3:10, 12; 4:11; 5:7, 9, 10, 12, 19.

## 1. *Salutation • James 1:1*

The author identifies himself as James, listing no qualifications or credentials. While he is a leader of the Jerusalem church and the brother of Jesus, he describes himself as a 'servant'. A more specific rendering would be *slave*. This particular sort of 'servant' cannot choose employment, but is bound. James identifies himself not by his familial tie with the Lord, but through his bonded servitude to him.[3]

While the phrase 'Lord Jesus Christ' (also see 2:1) suggests

3 Consider the contrast between 'slave' and 'free' in Galatians 3:28.

that the letter's recipients are Christians, the designation of 'the twelve tribes scattered among the nations' indicates that these particular Christians are Jews living outside their ancestral homeland. While 'Israel' alone could refer to non-Jews,[4] the phrase 'twelve tribes' particularly evokes the nation of Israel. The qualifier 'scattered among the nations' is the term *diaspora*, commonly used for the dispersion of the Jews among the Gentiles.[5] This entire designation suggests ethnic Jews scattered outside their ancestral homeland.

If the hearers of James are indeed Jews in the diaspora, they face marginalisation. They could have been forcibly scattered because of the persecution described in Acts 8:1–4 and 11:19. But whether they were forcibly relocated like modern-day refugees or willingly relocated like modern-day immigrants, they are minorities. Because they are Jewish, they are marginalised in their new lands.[6] They are also marginalised because they are Christ-followers during the infancy of the church. They live in pagan societies that do not support their Christ-centred values. They are likely treated differently and even discriminated against because of the way they dress, the way they speak, or their unusual names. Throughout this commentary, we will set the words of James within the context of the minority experience of these hearers, the twelve tribes scattered among the nations.

Notably, 'James' is the Greek form of 'Jacob'. James may be drawing on his name and using the designation 'twelve tribes'

4 See Romans 9:6–7 and Galatians 6:15–16, where Paul possibly redefines 'Israel' to go beyond the ethnic nation.

5 For example, John 7:35; Deuteronomy 30:4; Nehemiah 1:9; 2 Maccabees 1:27. Some consider diaspora in 1 Peter 1:1 to figuratively refer to Christians: both Jews and non-Jews. However, the specificity of 'twelve tribes' in James suggests that its recipients are indeed Jews.

6 On the marginalisation of diaspora Jews, see Moyer Hubbard, *Christianity in the Greco-Roman World: A Narrative Introduction* (Grand Rapids: Baker Academic, 2010), 24.

to invoke the type of relationship the patriarch Jacob had with his twelve sons, exhorting and directing them.

## *2. Trials lead to maturity • James 1:2–4*

Rather than a thanksgiving statement common to New Testament epistles (such as in Philippians 1:3; Philemon 4), James begins with a command. He exhorts his hearers to 'consider it pure joy' when they face trials. James is urging his hearers to have joy – not as an emotion from within, but as a conscious decision to consider something to be the case,[7] which results in gladdening. In other words, this is not a command to feel a certain way, but to think a certain way. Like Paul's command to 'take captive every thought' (2 Corinthians 10:5), this rejoicing takes discipline.

Regarding these trials, we must first establish what James is *not* writing about. These are not difficulties that come because of immoral actions, unwise decisions or lack of discipline. Modern examples might include being expelled from school for cheating, catching a disease from consensual sexual relations or losing a friend because we betrayed a secret.[8] These bring difficulties, but they are not what James has in mind. Furthermore, these trials do not reflect a belief akin to *karma*, the view that difficult circumstances come because of one's past evil deeds.

Rather, these trials in James 1:2 refer to difficulties that come by no fault of one's own. There is nothing one can do about these challenging situations. Generally, this sort of trial can include unexpected disease, unforeseen disasters and being persecuted because of one's faith.

---

7 Also see instances in Philippians 2:3; Hebrews 11:26; 2 Peter 1:13.

8 Donald R. Sunukjian, *Invitation to James: Persevering Through Trials to Win the Crown* (Wooster, OH: Weaver Book Company, 2014), 9.

The term for 'trials' can indicate either (a) difficult tests from outside oneself, or (b) temptations – enticements to give into sinful desires inside oneself. The fact that the hearers 'face' them indicates that the first type of test is in view. As minorities in their new lands, James's hearers are marginalised. Diaspora Jews often did not have access to certain rights and privileges.[9] These diverse trials are likely associated with their being different and underprivileged.

James 1:2 recalls Jesus's teaching about the vine and the vinedresser in John 15:2–3. There, he discusses fruitless branches and fruit-bearing ones. Jesus assures his disciples that they are already in the latter category. Fruit-bearing branches get pruned by the vinedresser. Like trials, pruning is unpleasant, but a Christ-follower is going through the painful process for their own good.

Trials often bring anger and sadness. Followers of Christ, when facing trials, may ask, 'Where is God in all of this? Doesn't God love me? How do I follow Jesus when life is so hard?' The hearers of James probably ask similar questions. Perhaps like modern immigrants, they are unable to access the more honourable professions they had in their previous homeland, and are relegated to the labour class. Perhaps their children are bullied for being different. Perhaps they are being cheated or harassed in the marketplaces.[10]

James addresses his hearers as 'my brothers and sisters', which he will use repeatedly. He characterises them as family members, communicating his emotional attachment to them. While the Greek only has the masculine *adelphoi*, the NIV's gender-inclusive 'brothers and sisters' is appropriate, since the default for a mixed group of men and women is the masculine form. Unless the

9 David A. deSilva, 'Jews in the Diaspora', in *The World of the New Testament: Cultural, Social, and Historical Contexts*, ed. Joel B. Green and Lee Martin McDonald (Grand Rapids: Baker Academic, 2013), 279.

10 See Sunukjian, *Invitation to James*, 8.

context indicates otherwise, the term 'brothers' generally refers to both male and female, fellow followers of Christ.

In James 1:3, our author states that these 'trials' are the 'testing of your faith'. Testing inherently includes an evaluation, a judgment about the object's worth. The term for 'testing' is largely used in both biblical (see 1 Peter 1:7; Psalm 12:6; Proverbs 27:21) and extrabiblical literature for precious metals in a fiery oven. This process was performed for two inextricable purposes: to test the metal for genuineness and to refine it for purity. The worth of a precious metal was often tied to the number of times it was fired: for example, silver 'purified seven times' (Psalm 12:6) is particularly pure.[11] The prevalence of this metallurgic practice suggests that James's hearers picture themselves being refined repeatedly in a fiery oven. This metallurgic imagery is more explicit in 1 Peter 1:6–7, which has several points of affinity with James 1:2–3.[12] Note that the act of testing implies an evaluator. As we will see in the associated saying in James 1:12, God does the testing and approving.

The object being tested is the hearers' faith. According to James, having joy in trials comes from the knowledge that their faith will be proved. Note that the Greek text for 'your' is specifically plural; this may indicate the faith of each of the readers, or a collective faith that they share. Together, the diaspora hearers are having their commitment to the Lord tested by the trials they face.

James 1:3 explains the remarkable exhortation in 1:2. The call to consider the trials to be *joy*, then, is not a command to have grit, to ignore the difficulties or to practise self-delusion. The

---

11 I make the case that metallurgic imagery is programmatic for James in Daniel K. Eng, '"The Refining of Your Faith"?: Metallurgic Testing Imagery in James', *Bulletin for Biblical Research* 32, no. 2 (2022): 182–201.

12 Also see 1 Corinthians 3:13, where the verb form conveys the fiery testing of one's work.

joy should be grounded in knowing and trusting the *future result* of their experiences. The hearers of James can rejoice in their trials because they expect that the testing produces perseverance.

In this context, perseverance means standing up under difficulty and enduring until the end. Perseverance is a common theme in the New Testament (for example, Matthew 24:13; 1 Thessalonians 1:3; Hebrews 10:36; Revelation 2:3). While many diaspora Jews abandoned their loyalty to their ancestral faith,[13] James urges steadfastness in faithfulness to Christ. He calls his hearers to endure, like an athlete perseveres through a race, keeping the goal in mind. They are to rejoice because persevering through their trials will ultimately lead to their good. This will be discussed in 1:12, where the 'crown of life' gives a picture of the end goal.

The value of perseverance may be especially appealing to eastern cultures influenced by Confucian values. Confucius taught that personal sacrifice, hard work and relational devotion lead to a harmonious society. However, in James, the value of perseverance is related to devotion to the Lord. Unlike Confucianism, the biblical call to perseverance is motivated not by this life, but by the life to come.

James 1:3–4 forms a chain-saying, with each clause repeating a previous word to emphasise the goal at the end.[14]

Testing → perseverance (1:3) → perseverance . . .
finish → mature and complete (1:4)

This chain has affinities with Romans 5:2–5 and 1 Peter 1:6–7. For each passage, the final element is set in the eschaton – the

13 Perhaps to gain social standing. See Hubbard, *Christianity in the Greco-Roman World*, 23.

14 The term rendered 'finish' is an adjective, *teleion* (woodenly the phrase is 'having a complete work'), which appears later, rendered 'mature' (*teleioi*).

end times. These parallels, as well as the eschatological content in James 1:12, suggest that 'mature and complete' in 1:4 is also set in the end times. The goal of the whole process is completion at the return of Christ.

The term for 'mature' is *teleioi*,[15] which often describes an undivided loyalty to God (Genesis 6:9; Deuteronomy 18:13; 1 Kings 11:4).[16] This usage fits with James, with the condemnation of the 'double-minded' (1:8, 4:8) and the challenge to choose God over the world (4:4). Note that 'mature' does not necessarily connote sinlessness. Rather, its pairing with 'complete' and the contrast with 'not lacking anything' indicates that the follower of Jesus can anticipate becoming a finished product.[17]

Just as physical fitness requires repeated discipline and exercise, so does the faith of these marginalised hearers of James. The trials are uncomfortable, but their repetition facilitates the maturity of faith; as Sam Allberry says, 'the Hollywood actor preparing to play the superhero does not become ready by lazing around . . . Muscle growth requires discomfort.'[18] Likewise, approaching trials with joy is a discipline.

For James's hearers, their difficulties will result in their good. The Baptist preacher Charles Spurgeon (1834–92) once preached, 'Had any other condition been better for you than the one in which you are, God would have put you there.'[19] Just as

---

15 *Telos* refers to a goal or end. The adjective occurs in Matthew 5:48 (NIV: 'perfect'), where Jesus calls for love like the Father's, which includes for one's enemies: it must be *complete*.

16 In the LXX. For a detailed discussion, see Allison, *James*, 155.

17 Davids calls this 'a rounding out as more and more "parts" of the righteous character are added'. See Davids, *Epistle of James*, 70.

18 Sam Allberry, *James for You: Showing You How Real Faith Looks in Real Life* (Epsom, Surrey: The Good Book Company, 2015), 14–15.

19 Charles Haddon Spurgeon, *Morning and Evening* (Carol Stream, IL: Hendrickson, 2010), 633.

the prophet Habakkuk concludes, even amid the most difficult circumstances, the follower of Jesus can be joyful in God (Habakkuk 3:17–18).

James 1:2–4, as part of the prologue, introduces the concept of testing, which will be revisited in 1:12–14 and also in 2:21, an Old Testament allusion. This subunit also introduces the concepts of faith (James 2:14–26), perseverance (1:12, 25; 5:11), completeness (1:15, 17, 25; 2:8, 22; 3:2; 5:11) and work/deeds (1:25; 2:9, 14–26; 3:13; 5:16).

## *3. Single-mindedly asking God for wisdom • James 1:5–8*

The catchword 'lack' connects the previous saying to this one, but James shifts the topic. As the minority hearers of James experience trials, they need wisdom for responding. James urges them to continually seek this wisdom from God.[20]

This 'wisdom' is from God; it is not human wisdom. As the early church theologian Augustine (354–430 AD) points out, 'If this wisdom were from us, it would not come down from above, nor would it have to be asked for from God who created us.'[21] James will discuss human wisdom and heavenly wisdom in 3:13–18.

In 1:5, James characterises God as generous, who 'gives generously to all without finding fault'. While many people, both ancient and modern, give gifts based on the recipient's merit, God gives without reservations. James's declaration, 'it will be given', echoes Jesus's and Paul's description of God's generosity (Matthew 7:7; Philippians 4:19). If God were serving a meal,

20 'Ask' holds the force of a command, with the tense suggesting a continuous prayer.

21 Augustine, *On the Free Choice of the Will, On Grace and Free Choice, and Other Writings*, trans. Peter King (Cambridge: Cambridge University Press, 2010), 184.

he would heap out lavish portions of rich fare to all who ask, without discrimination. This wisdom is a good gift that God is eager to give.

In James 1:6, the requestor of wisdom must 'believe and not doubt'. On the surface, this condition seems difficult to meet. After all, every follower of Jesus has questions about their faith. Is James teaching that we are doomed to have our prayers unanswered if we have any doubts?

The rest of James 1:6–8 offers us some guidance. First, James is describing someone who is divided in loyalty. While the NIV warns to 'not doubt', the verb here refers to making distinctions and division, or disputing with someone.[22] Given the verb's contrast with faith and its usage in 2:4, this person is 'divided in purpose'.[23] He has not settled on where his allegiance lies, but is 'double-minded' (1:8; see 4:8). A fitting adjective for this divided, double nature is *duplicitous*.[24] The 'double-minded' person may not be attempting to deceive, but nevertheless has duplicity in their loyalty, wavering back and forth (see 1 Kings 18:21). The stakes of this 'doubting' are much higher than wavering when supporting different sports teams. James will later state that their disloyalty to God has made them God's enemies (4:4).

Second, faith in James 1:6 does not refer to initial conversion or intellectual agreement to theological statements. Rather, as we will discuss, it describes a committed adherence to God. The person who has divided loyalty would dispute with God, not being faithfully committed to him. Thus, it is best to see the

22 Henry George Liddell and Robert Scott, 'Διακρίνω', in LSJ.

23 The verb's middle voice suggests that someone is disputing within oneself, i.e., wavering. For more on this verb, see Stanley E. Porter and Chris S. Stevens, 'Doubting BDAG on Doubt: A Lexical Examination of Διακρίνω and Its Theological Ramifications', *Filología Neotestamentaria* 30 (2017): 43–70.

24 Elsa Tamez, *The Scandalous Message of James: Faith without Works Is Dead* (New York: Crossroad, 2002), 56–7.

manner of wisdom-asking to be *in committed faithfulness, not divided in purpose.*

James describes the divided-disputing person as a wave that is wind-tossed. Consider a small rowing boat on the sea during a violent storm. There is no stability, no anchor to keep it from being tossed around. The apostle Paul gives a similar image of immature believers being tossed back and forth (Ephesians 4:14). The double-minded person is 'consistently inconsistent',[25] and 'cannot decide with whom his allegiance lies'.[26] This descriptor for 'double-minded' also occurs in 4:8, where it is associated with rebellion against God. The duplicitous individual, as James states, must 'not expect to receive anything from the Lord'.

What is the remedy for double-mindedness? It is having a single adherence, an unwavering commitment. The author of Hebrews, perhaps following the image of being tossed back and forth, calls the eternal hope in God 'an anchor for the soul' (Hebrews 6:19). Being fully committed to God results in singleness and stability. It is this undivided person who will receive wisdom from the generous Giver.

I remember walking on a passenger bridge about to board an aeroplane. The middle-aged man walking next to me suddenly turned to me and said that it was his first time flying. Since he looked nervous, I assured him that he had chosen a good airline. As we got to the doorway, he stopped. As he stared at the small space between the jet bridge and the plane, I could tell he was contemplating his commitment. With some encouragement from the flight attendant, he finally stepped onto the jet. He stopped wavering and made the full commitment. Similarly, James challenges his hearers not to go back and forth between opposing loyalties and to commit singly to God. Followers of

25 Blomberg and Kamell, *James*, 54.

26 Daniel K. Eng, *James: An Honor–Shame Paraphrase*, ed. Jayson Georges (USA: Timé Press, 2018), 12.

Christ must fully step off the passenger bridge and onto a stable, reliable vehicle.

As part of the prologue, James 1:5–8 contains several concepts that will be repeated later in the epistle: generosity (1:16–18; 2:14–15), prayer (4:2–3; 5:13–18) and a condemnation of the 'double-minded' (4:8).

## *4. The great reversal • James 1:9–11*

This section builds on the previous content,[27] with a contrast between the double-minded and the humble brother. Here, James shows a dichotomy between a lowly believer and a rich person.

The term for 'believer' indicates that this humble person is a follower of Jesus. The 'humble circumstances' contrasts those who are rich (1:10), making the state of material lowliness explicit. Also, 'humble' does not just point to lack of riches, but also to disadvantaged status. As ethnic and religious minorities, James's hearers are at the bottom of the social ladder, unlikely to have much influence. The rich, on the other hand, are at the top of the ladder; they have the financial means to exploit others and the influence to use the legal system to their advantage (see 2:6–7; 5:4–6).[28]

While the context indicates material wealth and earthly status, there is an ethical element to being 'lowly'. In the Old Testament, those who seek the Lord are portrayed as needy, and the Lord favours them (for example, Psalm 86:1; Jeremiah 20:13; Isaiah 41:17). Jesus calls himself 'humble' (Matthew 11:29), and Mary

---

27 The Greek particle *de* signals development of previous content.

28 For a discussion of the social and ethical dimensions of poverty in the New Testament, see Bruce J. Malina and Richard L. Rohrbaugh, *Social-Science Commentary on the Synoptic Gospels*, (Second edition; Minneapolis: Augsburg, 2002), 48–9.

describes the humble with favour (Luke 1:51–3). With their lack of resources and social influence, the lowly are likely to seek God for provision and justice. By contrast, the rich are more likely to be functional atheists, acting as if God does not exist (see James 4:15–16; 5:4). Thus, James is likely urging his hearers to continue embodying humility before the Lord, as he teaches in 4:6–10.

While 'humble' and 'rich' are earthly circumstances, their reversal is not earthly. In reality, the rich of this world are constantly getting richer, and the poor are getting poorer. Also, if earthly poverty led to earthly exaltation, we would not need to care for the poor (see 1:27; 2:14–16). Why care for the poor if they currently have an advantage? Rather, the results are eschatological, happening in the afterlife. The description of the humiliation of the rich in 1:10–11 points to an irreversible demise: they will pass away, wither and be destroyed.[29] These sayings find parallels in the sayings of Jesus:[30]

| | **James 1:9–10** | **Matthew 20:16; Luke 13:30** |
|---|---|---|
| Shame | humble circumstances | The last |
| Honour | high position | will be first |
| Honour | rich | and the first |
| Shame | humiliation | will be last |

29 James 1:9–11 shares terms with Isaiah 40:2–9, which describes an eschatological reversal. See Davids, *Epistle of James*, 77; Klyne R. Snodgrass, 'Streams of Tradition Emerging from Isaiah 40:1–5 and Their Adaptation in the New Testament', *Journal for the Study of the New Testament* 2 (1980): 24–45.

30 Allison, *James*, 199. Also see the same terms in Luke 14:11.

In these and other teachings (Matthew 18:4; 19:14; Luke 6:20–23; 22:26; Mark 10:15), Jesus describes an end-time honouring of the disadvantaged, often called the *great reversal*. The minority hearers of James, facing trials and being disadvantaged, can expect eternal reward.

But what about the rich in James 1:10–11? The context suggests that the rich are not among the epistle's hearers. To describe the rich, he does not use 'believer' (the same term in plural form is 'brothers and sisters' elsewhere in James), which appeared in 1:9 for the lowly person. Also, James largely describes the rich as wicked (2:5–6; 5:1–6). In fact, the description of their ruin echoes the psalmist's description of the wicked (Psalm 1:4–6).

How can the rich 'take pride' in their demise?[31] This boasting is not true; it is ironic. While they are enjoying their wealth now, their eternal destruction is coming (see 5:1). In the tone of a prophetic oracle, James declares doom on the rich; there is no warning for the rich to repent.

In James 1:2–3, the author's declaration to persevere through trial is unexpected. Consistent with that exhortation, he describes the future destruction of the rich to encourage his Christ-following hearers.[32] The audience is called to stay faithful, even while experiencing difficulties. This is consistent with the epistle's thesis statement (1:12), which we will examine below.

As part of the letter's prologue, James 1:9–11 introduces concepts that will be repeated later in the epistle. The eschatological content is explicit here, and James will repeatedly discuss eschatological judgment. Also, he introduces the concept of favour on the poor (1:27; 2:5), the concept of humility (4:6–10), the

---

31 'Take pride' (NIV, James 1:10) is not in the Greek text. But it is in verse 9, and so inferred from there.

32 For an analysis of the views about the identity of the rich in James 1:9–11, see René Krüger, *Der Jakobusbrief als prophetische Kritik der Reichen: Eine exegetische Untersuchung aus lateinamerikanischer Perspektive* (Münster: Lit, 2005), 126–30.

ephemeral nature of wealth (4:15–16; 5:2–6) and the condemnation of the wicked rich (5:1–6).

## 5. *The approved will receive the crown of life* • *James 1:12*

As discussed above, James 1:12 is not only the key saying in the prologue of James, but it also serves as a thesis statement for the epistle. It has connections with the beginning (1:2–4) and the end of the prologue (1:25), as well as the end of the body of James (5:11). With the concept of judgment dispersed throughout the epistle, the saying in 1:12 sums up the epistle's message that those who are tested and approved will be rewarded in the end.

James 1:12 continues the pattern of 1:2–11, with a positive relationship between affirmed behaviour and future reward. Like the previous content, this reward is set in the eschaton. As we will see below, this saying also connects to the next section through the terms for *trial* and *tempted*, which are in the same word family.

The statement of blessing is a macarism, a biblical saying which congratulates someone who displays the desired behaviour (such as Job 5:17; Psalm 1:1; Proverbs 14:21). The most relevant macarisms for James are in the Sermon on the Mount (Matthew 5:3–12). Like the Matthean Beatitudes, James 1:12 follows the formula of 'blessed' and a subject, followed by a clause explaining the reason for the state of blessing.[33]

A crown is a visible adornment for a person's high status or esteem. A poignant example is the crown that Mordecai wears in his public celebration (Esther 8:15). With the qualifier 'of

33 For how macarisms communicate human flourishing within right relationship with God, see Jonathan T. Pennington, *The Sermon on the Mount and Human Flourishing: A Theological Commentary* (Grand Rapids: Baker Academic, 2017), 41–67.

life', the crown in James is revealed to be life itself – a more explicit rendering would be *the crown that is life*.[34] A notable parallel is Revelation 2:10, where Christ promises a 'crown of life' (NIV: 'life as your victor's crown') to the one who is faithful until death. In the context of James 1:12, this 'life' is the future eschatological life. This is eternal life with the eternal God,[35] as described in the sayings of Jesus (for example, Mark 10:30; John 5:24). Thus, those who persevere in single faithfulness to God can look forward to eternal life.

The image of an adornment of esteem is especially poignant to these diaspora Jesus-followers. Far away from their homeland, they are reminded of the exile owing to their ancestors' apostasy. They are also far away from the Temple, making it difficult for them to express their faith like their kinsmen in the homeland. James assures them that, despite their shameful distance from the land, they can look forward to future honour.

Also, as minorities, the hearers of James experience marginalisation. They are not the ones to whom their societies predominantly cater. Modern minorities are constantly reminded that they are different from what their societies value. The marketplace, advertisements and mass media reveal that minorities are outside what is considered influential, good and beautiful. But James's declaration in 1:12 offers encouragement to those experiencing marginalisation: they can receive eternal esteem as they are valued by their Creator.

As we will continue to discuss, there is a correlation in James between God's faithful people and the poor. This is consistent with the concept that those who are underprivileged now will be exalted later. Likewise, as 1:10–11 has introduced, those who are esteemed by the world will be lost – or the least – later.

---

34 See A. K. M. Adam, *James: A Handbook on the Greek Text* (Waco, TX: Baylor University Press, 2013), 14.

35 Aída Besançon Spencer, *A Commentary on James* (Grand Rapids: Kregel Academic, 2020), 74.

James's hearers are encouraged to wait patiently (see 5:7) for this reversal to occur.

James describes the blessed in several ways. First, they are the ones who persevere under trial (1:2–4). Rather than abandon God, they continue in loyal allegiance to him. This is the sort of faith affirmed in 1:6. Rather than being double-minded (1:8), they display a single-minded loyalty.

Second, the blessed will stand the test. In other words, they will prove to be loyal. This is another connection with the opening command in 1:2–4.[36] They are 'tried and true' or 'approved'. With the language of 1:2–4 (see the commentary there) indicating a connection with the testing of precious metals, this 'test' implies an evaluator. Here in James 1:12, God's eschatological judgment is explicit. Those who persevere, who do not turn their backs on God in their trials, will be approved by God in the end, and they will receive their crowns.

Third, the blessed love the Lord. Persevering through trial demonstrates their commitment to God. At Sinai, the Lord declared that those who love him would keep his commandments (Exodus 20:6). More significantly, this phrase recalls the *Shema*, the renowned call to Israel to love God in Deuteronomy 6:5. The saying in James 1:12 also echoes Deuteronomy 30:19–20, as those who love the Lord and hold fast to him will receive life. Despite their distance from the land and the Temple, these diaspora Jewish Christians are encouraged that – if they persevere – they will be rewarded in the end.

Several of James's programmatic themes come up in 1:12. The concepts of enduring through trial and an eschatological reward are reinforced here. This will appear throughout James, but most explicitly in 5:11, which will conclude the main body of the epistle.

36 'Stood the test' is *dokimos*, a cognate of *dokimion* in 1:3. The adjective, examples of which are found in Romans 16:10 and 2 Timothy 2:15, denotes someone (or something) who has gone through evaluation and has passed the test.

# 3

# Prologue 2: Temptation, Being Quick to Hear and Slow to Anger

## JAMES 1:13–27

The modern teacher can teach this subunit of the introductory prologue as a standalone teaching unit. It would be prudent to refer back to the thesis statement at 1:12, since it forms an *inclusio* with 1:25. As we will discuss, James 1:13–27 introduces concepts and terms that will be repeated later in the epistle.

**13**When tempted, no one should
say, 'God is tempting me.' For God
cannot be tempted by evil, nor does
he tempt anyone; **14**but each person is
tempted when they are dragged away
by their own evil desire and enticed.
**15**Then, after desire has conceived, it
gives birth to sin; and sin, when it is
full-grown, gives birth to death.

**16**Don't be deceived, my dear
brothers and sisters. **17**Every good
and perfect gift is from above,
coming down from the Father of
the heavenly lights, who does not
change like shifting shadows. **18**He
chose to give us birth through the
word of truth, that we might be a
kind of firstfruits of all he created.

*Listening and doing*

**19**My dear brothers and sisters,
take note of this: everyone should
be quick to listen, slow to speak and
slow to become angry, **20**because
human anger does not produce
the righteousness that God desires.
**21**Therefore, get rid of all moral filth
and the evil that is so prevalent, and
humbly accept the word planted in
you, which can save you.

**22**Do not merely listen to the word,
and so deceive yourselves. Do what
it says. **23**Anyone who listens to the
word but does not do what it says is
like someone who looks at his face
in a mirror **24**and, after looking at
himself, goes away and immediately

forgets what he looks like. **25** But whoever looks intently into the perfect law that gives freedom and continues in it - not forgetting what they have heard but doing it - they will be blessed in what they do.

**26** Those who consider themselves religious and yet do not keep a tight rein on their tongues deceive themselves, and their religion is worthless. **27** Religion that God our Father accepts as pure and faultless is this: to look after orphans and widows in their distress and to keep oneself from being polluted by the world.

## *1. Temptation is not from God • James 1:13–18*

After the thesis statement in 1:12, James continues the prologue, shifting from the topic of external trials to another sort of test. In 1:13–18, James discusses enticement towards unrighteous behaviour: temptation.[1]

Note the logic of this subsection. The section starts with a command, like 1:5 and 1:9. James prohibits his hearers from stating that the source of the temptation is God. He corrects this faulty thinking by describing the character of God in 1:13b. After that, he indicates the true source of temptation in 1:14–15. Finally, 1:16–18 elaborates on God's character and the history of the people.

James 1:13b describes God's character by disassociating him from evil. God never engages in evil behaviours, nor does he desire to do them. Here, James gives a theodicy – a defence of God's character in the presence of evil. With 'no one' and 'anyone', James makes clear the separation between God and evil.

Some might wonder about instances in Scripture where God appears to 'test' people. For example, God 'tested' Abraham (Genesis 22:1) and 'tested' the hearts of the people (Deuteronomy

1 The catchword *peirasmon* (NIV: 'trial') in 1:12 connects to its cognate *peirazomenos* (NIV: 'tempted') in 1:13.

8:2). There is also Jesus being led out to the wilderness to be tempted by the devil (Matthew 4:1). Space does not allow for a full treatment here, but these occurrences are compatible with James's message. The context of James's teaching reveals that the *intent* of temptation here is to lure a person to sin. God does not desire evil, and he does not tempt in this sense. Rather, God tests people, looking for allegiance and obedience.

Also relevant is the Lord's Prayer, which includes a plea that God would 'lead us not into temptation' (Matthew 6:13). While the term rendered 'temptation' has a range of meaning, the term is likely being used in the same way as in James 1:12, to refer to external trial[2] rather than an enticement to sin. Whether these trials occur in the end (see eschatological elements in the Sermon on the Mount) or are general times of trying pressure, the Lord's Prayer asks God to spare the disciple from difficulties.[3]

In James 1:14–15, our author states that the true source of temptation is not God, but one's evil desires. With 'dragged away' and 'enticed', James uses vivid imagery of an animal baited into a trap or a fish drawn by a lure. Temptations to sin always come with bait – something that seems desirable to our evil inclinations. Our illicit desires are the cause of our temptations.

I remember moving to California after being licensed to drive in Massachusetts. To transfer my licence, I needed to complete a written traffic exam. At the Department of Motor Vehicles, the clerk tried to hand me a California driver's manual so I could study it. 'No thanks!' I confidently told the clerk. I was convinced that the exam would be a piece of cake; I did not need to study.

After completing the exam, I got my results within a few minutes. The same clerk reported to me that I had failed the

2 Also see its usage in Acts 20:19; Galatians 4:14; 2 Peter 2:9.

3 See John Nolland, *The Gospel of Matthew* (Grand Rapids: Eerdmans, 2005), 292.

exam and that I would have to take it again. With an amused look on her face, she handed me the driver's manual.

Failing the traffic exam was my fault. I did not adequately prepare. I cannot blame the exam for my failure. Its intent was not to trap me, but to test me. In the same way, James teaches that people cannot blame God for temptations to sin. God is not intending us to sin. While our circumstances may be the setting for our temptations, the temptations come about because of our wicked longings.

James then continues with more imagery, shifting to birthing. The evil desire gives birth to sin,[4] which grows up to give birth to death. This death, in contrast to the eternal life in 1:12, is eschatological. It is the grave result of temptation: if followed, it will lead to eternal destruction (see Romans 6:23). James warns his hearers not to let this life cycle begin.

Just like trials, temptations to sin will come. The disadvantaged hearers of James may be tempted to immoral acts for relief from their difficulties: deceiving, cheating, or stealing. Temptations serve as a test of one's faith – will one be dragged away and give birth to sin? Or will one disassociate from evil and persevere in allegiance to God?

Next, James urges his hearers not to believe the lie that evil comes from God. After all, he is the source of 'every good and perfect gift'. Again, James appears to echo Jesus's words in the Sermon on the Mount (Matthew 7:11): God gives gifts that are good.

James 1:17b–18 describes God in three ways. First, he is 'the Father of the heavenly lights', the Creator of the sun, moon and stars (see Psalm 136:7). Likewise, the Father is the source of blessings 'coming down' from above. With the paganism and

4 See imagery of the birthing of sin in Job 15:35; Psalm 7:14; Isaiah 59:4.

differing beliefs about origins around them, this designation is significant to the diaspora Jews.[5]

Second, James highlights God's immutability: he 'does not change like shifting shadows' (see Malachi 3:6). Unlike the unstable person in 1:6–8, God is not double-minded. The single-minded generosity of God, introduced in 1:5, is reprised here.

Third, in James 1:18, God is described as the source of good things. The birthing imagery here creates a stark contrast to the birthing of sin and death in 1:14–15. God is described as both a father and a (birthing) mother in 1:17–18, illustrating his multifaceted goodness. He is the source of good things, and prominently births 'us'. The purpose of this birthing is made clear: 'that we might be a kind of firstfruits of all he created'.

Who is the 'us' that God birthed? While there are several interpretations,[6] the best fit is probably Christians (see James 2:1; 1 Peter 1:3, 23), particularly those of the twelve tribes (see 1:1).[7] God has provided a good gift (1:18) to those who follow Jesus: eternal life.

With 'firstfruits', James indicates that there will be further reaping. There is more to come! The diaspora hearers of the epistle are just the beginning: there will be other people(s) who will join them (see Revelation 14:4). They are minorities and marginalised now, but God's work is not done. This is a possible allusion to non-Jews joining the church, for which we must rejoice.

Continuing the prologue, James 1:13–18 revisits the generosity of God (1:5). This is seen in the crown of life (1:12), and later

5 For more on Jewish distinctiveness in the diaspora, see deSilva, 'Diaspora', 284–7.

6 The major views are (a) all of humankind, (b) Israel as God's people, or (c) Christians. For proponents of each, see (respectively) L. E. Elliott-Binns, 'James I. 18: Creation or Redemption?', *New Testament Studies* 3 (1957): 154–5; Allison, *James*, 282; Dibelius, *James*, 90.

7 See Varner, *James*, 98.

in the giving of the kingdom (2:5) and of grace to the humble (4:6). Also, James continues the focus on eschatological fates, describing death (1:15) in contrast to eternal life. James also introduces new motifs: sin (2:9; 4:8, 17; 5:15–20), evil desires (2:1–6; 3:14–16; 4:1–4) and death (2:26; 3:8; 5:20).

## 2. *Quick to hear, slow to speak, slow to anger • James 1:19–25*

James repeats 'my dear brothers and sisters', addressing Christ-followers who are beloved to him. After affirming that God does not desire sin but is the source of good things,[8] James gives an alternative to sin in 1:19–25: behaving righteously. He continues the motif of the word of God in 1:18, 1:21 and 1:23. Also, the concept of 'planted in you' may relate to the birthing imagery of 1:15 and 1:18.[9]

James 1:19 contains a threefold command for living righteously. Each of the three parts is developed in the content following:

| **Command** | **Development** |
|---|---|
| Quick to listen | 1:22–5 |
| Slow to speak | 1:26 |
| Slow to become angry | 1:20–21 |

8 The Greek conjunction *de* signals development from previous material.

9 Ursula Ulrike Kaiser, '"Receive the Innate Word That Is Able to Save You" (Jas 1:21b): Soteriology in the Epistle of James', in *Sōtēria: Salvation in Early Christianity and Antiquity*, ed. David S. du Toit, Christine Gerber and Christiane Zimmermann (Leiden: Brill, 2019), 464.

## 'Slow to anger'

The third part is expanded first. The phrase 'slow to anger' echoes an oft-repeated description of the Lord in the Old Testament (for example, Exodus 34:6; Psalm 86:15; Joel 2:13). It is not an indication of never getting angry; rather, it is a delay or reluctance towards anger. The hearers of James, facing difficulties as minorities in a hostile world, would be tempted to anger, to take vengeance or to mistreat others. But James calls them to reflect God's character, showing patience or endurance (see James 5:10) amid difficulty.

While wisdom literature warns its hearers to be slow to anger (Proverbs 16:32; Ecclesiastes 7:9), James gives an explicit motivation in 1:20: 'human anger does not produce the righteousness that God desires'. The latter could refer to righteous character, of which God approves,[10] or it could refer to a right standing before God.[11] Either way, it is clearly what God desires. He is the source, standard and judge of righteousness. With the commands in 1:19 and 1:21, James urges his hearers to behave in a way that will bring a favourable judgment in the end.

In the context of righteousness, James exhorts his minority hearers to accept the 'word planted in you'. This recalls the biblical imagery of new birth (1 Peter 1:3–4; John 3:3) and the placement of the law into the hearts of God's people (Hebrews 10:16; Jeremiah 31:33). James describes God planting his word – the gospel and his ethics into his followers.[12] This word can 'save' – adherence leads to eschatological life. By accepting the word and following it, the hearers of James expect to have

10 See, for example, James Hardy Ropes, *A Critical and Exegetical Commentary on the Epistle of St. James* (Edinburgh: T&T Clark, 1916), 170; Patrick J. Hartin, *James* (Collegeville, MN: Liturgical Press, 2003), 96.

11 See McKnight, *Letter of James*, 139.

12 Kaiser, 'Innate Word', 469.

righteousness. Having been tested, they will have their esteem with God in the end (1:12).

James makes 'accept his word' more specific. First, they must 'get rid of all moral filth and the evil'. As if they were stripping off clothing, the hearers are to remove their vices.[13] Human anger is part of that moral filth, the sin that is birthed by temptation and evil desire (1:15). Second, in contrast to anger, James exhorts his hearers to receive the word 'humbly'.[14] One who accepts the word in meekness will submit to it, bringing about the righteousness that God desires.

## 'Quick to listen'

In James 1:22–5, the development of 'be quick to listen' has a chiastic structure:

1:22 Do what the word says, not just listen.
  1:23–4 The one who only listens is one who looks in a mirror and forgets.
1:25 Do not forget the law, but do it.

After James likens the one who just listens to the forgetful mirror-user, he states that one who continues (or perseveres) in the law is 'blessed'. As discussed above, this repeats the key terms found in the thesis statement in 1:12. In the context of James 1, this blessing for the faithful is the hope of eschatological life.

---

13 This theme occurs with Joshua removing his filthy clothes in Zechariah 3:3–5. See David P. Nystrom, *James* (Grand Rapids: Zondervan, 2011), 92. Also see similar imagery in Ephesians 4:22, 25; Colossians 3:8; Hebrews 12:1; 1 Peter 2:1.

14 This term is not a cognate of the term describing the humble circumstances described in 1:9. Here, the context indicates that this term describes an attitude of meekness.

James again urges his hearers to follow God and his word to receive a favourable judgment in the end.

The command to 'listen' likely reminds the diaspora hearers of the *Shema* (Deuteronomy 6:4). The call to 'hear' introduces the command for the people to obey the teachings and to teach them to their children. It is not enough to listen to the word; mental assent is inadequate. James teaches that his hearers must 'do what it says'. James's command to be quick to listen implies a readiness to act. The inseparable connection between 'listening' and 'doing' recurs throughout biblical literature (for example, Exodus 24:7; 2 Kings 14:11; Matthew 13:23; 18:15–16; Luke 9:35).

Like Jesus and Paul (see Matthew 7:24, 26; Romans 2:13), James communicates that merely hearing the word is not enough. I would suspect that most people believe flossing their teeth is essential to dental hygiene. However, many of the same folks would admit to doing it less often than they should. Knowing the truth is not enough; it is action that counts. Similarly, it is not enough that we acknowledge the biblical truth. We must put it into practice.

In 1:22, James uses a label: be 'doers' rather than merely 'hearers'. A 'hearer' in this instance describes someone in the audience of a public speaker.[15] Graeco-Roman philosophers would often draw crowds to listen to them. James, however, urges his own audience to do more than just hear the word of God. After all, one who merely hears the word is deceiving himself. Like the doers – the artisans, authors and composers they would see in the marketplaces[16] – James's hearers were to put their knowledge into practice (see Romans 2:13). Again, James echoes Jesus's words from the Sermon on the Mount (Matthew 7:24), describing someone who not only hears but practises.

The imagery of the mirror is apt. After all, what is the mirror's

15 'Ἀκροᾱτής', in LSJ.
16 'Ποιητής', in LSJ.

use if knowing your appearance doesn't lead to action? I recall a preacher using similar imagery.[17] While attending a party, he saw his reflection in the bathroom. He was mortified to see an unusually long hair coming out of his nostril. It must have grown while coiled up in his nose and suddenly made its way out. Upon seeing it, he could have gone back to the party without doing anything about it. But he wisely removed his long nose hair.

Like the word of God, the mirror truthfully gives its user information upon which to act. The 'law', synonymous with the 'word' in 1:22, is described in two ways. First, the law is 'perfect', which also describes God's gifts (1:17). The law is not lacking anything, and its source is the Father. Second, the law gives freedom. It is not a licence to rebel against God, but the ability to live in submission to him. The Christ-follower is freed from slavery to sin to fulfil Christ's law (see Romans 8:2; Galatians 6:2; 1 Corinthians 9:21; 1 Peter 2:16).[18] The one who looks intently into the law should 'continue' in it. This verb, related to 'persevere' in 1:3–4 and 1:12, conveys faithfulness to the word through action. In accordance with the thesis statement (1:12), this constancy of allegiance will result in eschatological blessing (also see John 13:17).

The hearers of James, far from their ancestral homeland, can have the esteem of being called doers of the word. Like the wise man who built his house on the rock, the ones who practise the word of God will have life when the eschaton comes; the ones who do not will perish like the foolish man inside his collapsing home (Matthew 7:24–7).

As part of the prologue, James 1:19–25 introduces several motifs that will recur: speech ethics (2:12; 4:11; 5:12), doing the word (2:14–26), righteousness and justification (2:21–5; 3:18; 5:6; 5:16) and eschatological salvation (2:14; 4:12; 5:20).

---

17 Revd Cory Ishida, Evergreen Baptist Church of San Gabriel Valley, personal communication.

18 Peter H. Davids, *James* (Peabody, MA: Hendrickson, 1989), 25.

## *3. Religion accepted by God • James 1:26–7*

James 1:26 connects with the previous subsection, since it develops the command to be 'slow to speak' in 1:19. However, it forms a pair of complementary statements with 1:27, creating a contrast between 'worthless' and acceptable religion. The term rendered 'religion' describes commitment to God; one might substitute a term like *worship* or *piety*.

'Worthless' religion describes that of a person who does not control their tongue. The word of God teaches prudence in when and how to speak (see, for example, Psalm 34:12–13; Proverbs 10:19; Ephesians 4:29; 1 Peter 3:8–10). The one who does not control the tongue does not adhere to the wisdom of God, like the man who looks in the mirror and forgets his appearance. It is a dangerous thing to hear the word of God but to not practise it. They may say they are 'religious' or faithful, but they are deceiving themselves (see 1:16): such 'religion' is worthless in the sight of God.

James describes having a rein on one's tongue, like using a bridle on a horse. The command is not to refrain from speaking; a rein does not immobilise an animal. Rather, just like a bridle exercises control, the command is to be slow to speak. This imagery of the bridling for the tongue will be used again in James 3. One must control the tongue, because it is capable of great evil. The connection with human anger (1:19) is apt here: people often have the most difficult time controlling their tongues when they are angry.

After describing worthless religion, in 1:27 James describes what the Father accepts as 'pure and faultless'. The twofold description describes both outward acts of compassion and personal piety.

First, James states that acceptable faithfulness is to look after the fatherless and widows. Caring for the less fortunate is an expression of one's worship (see Mark 10:21; Romans 15:26).[19] In addition to their destitution, widows and orphans were of the lowest social class. The call to associate with them is set in contrast with showing favouritism to the rich in the next section (2:2–4).

Remarkably, the Old Testament sayings about the fatherless and widows usually also include 'foreigners' (for example, Exodus 22:21–2; Deuteronomy 10:18; Psalm 146:9; Jeremiah 7:6; 22:3; Ezekiel 22:7). The omission of 'foreigners' in James indicates that these diaspora hearers are themselves the foreigners. While also marginalised and disadvantaged, they are called to care for orphans and widows as an expression of devotion to God.

Second, James states that acceptable religion is 'to keep oneself from being polluted by the world'. The moral concept of being rid of filth (1:21) is revisited here: one's inner life should reflect worship. Just like a person should eat the right foods to be healthy, a follower of Jesus should be vigilant about what influences them. James's usage of 'world' here is consistent with a New Testament theme: one should not conform to the ways of the world (for example, Romans 12:2; Ephesians 2:2; 1 John 2:15–17). Just like fish must swim against the current to have oxygen flow through their gills, the hearers of James must go against the world's ways.

James exhorts his hearers, who are far away from the Temple, that they can still express devotion to God. They are an unfamiliar people in an unfamiliar place, facing the influences of Greek philosophies and paganism. Followers of Christ should not seek joy in the world. Rather, they are to rejoice (1:2) that their perseverance will result in eternal reward (1:12).

James 1:26–7 introduces several topics, including a rein on the

---

19 The Jerusalem church, of which James is a prominent figure, is the one that receives the collection from the saints in Macedonia and Achaia through Paul. See 1 Corinthians 6:1–4; 2 Corinthians 8:1–5; Romans 15:24–32.

tongue (3:2–12) and a dichotomy between God and the world (4:1–10). One might consider James 1:26–7 to be a reversed table of contents for the content immediately following: the major concepts of reining the tongue (3:1–12) and caring for the poor (2:1–26).[20]

20 Francis, 'Form and Function', 118.

# 4

# Structure of James 2

As we begin the body of James, we have another grand *inclusio* bracketed by 2:12–13 and 4:11–12.[1] The first section of James 2, as we will see, is a preview of the next content. We have already discussed the grand *inclusio* that characterises the entire epistle (1:12 and 5:11).

There are clusters of repeated terms at both 2:12–13 and 4:11–12, both occurring at points of transition in the epistle. First, the leading parallel is a cluster of terms for *judge*, *judgment* and *judging*. Aside from a related term in 3:1,[2] there are no intervening instances of these terms. Both texts point to God as the sole rightful judge, and the readers are not to take on his role. Second, 'law' occurs five times in 2:8–12 and four times in 4:11 (with 'Lawgiver' in 4:12), with no intervening occurrences.[3] Third, both passages contain content about acting in obedience or keeping the law. Fourth, both address speech ethics, with 'speak' (2:12) and 'slander' (4:11). Fifth, 'neighbour' occurs in 4:12 rather than his more common 'brothers and sisters'. The term 'neighbour' recalls the love-command from Leviticus 19.18, occurring in 2:8. If 2:12 serves as a summary of 2:1–11, 'neighbour' is another connection between 2:12–13 and 4:11–12.

The *inclusio* brackets together content that urges the hearers of James to live in adherence to God, in expectation of eschatological judgment. In other words, the exhortations of James

1 See George H. Guthrie and Mark E. Taylor, 'The Structure of James', *Catholic Biblical Quarterly* 68 (2006): 684–5; Eng, *Eschatological Approval*, 73–4.

2 'Judgment' in 2:12 is *krisis*, while the term in 3:1 is *krima*.

3 Mark Edward Taylor, *A Text-Linguistic Investigation into the Discourse Structure of James* (London: T&T Clark, 2006), 64.

2:14–4:10 teach that obedience and allegiance will result in a favourable end-time verdict. This is compatible with the larger *inclusio* between 1:12 and 5:11.

James 2 has two large movements. The logic of each movement progresses from a specific example to a general principle. The first section (2:1–13), which serves as a bridge from the prologue to the body, starts with the prohibition of favouritism and moves to the general exhortation of adhering to the whole law. The second section (2:14–26), which starts the body of James, begins with a rhetorical question and widens to discuss the larger point that faith without deeds is dead.

# 5

# Eschewing Favouritism, Obeying the Law

## JAMES 2:1–13

James 2:1–13 serves as the introduction of the body of James, which culminates in the opening of the large *inclusio*. This section is a bridge between the prologue and the rest of James, having parallels with both 1:1–27 and the section following it, 2:14–27.[1] All three themes introduced in 1:26–7 recur in 2:1–13: use of the tongue (2:3, 12), caring for the poor (2:2–6) and eschewing the ways of the world (not showing favouritism, 2:1–9).[2] Also, James 2:13 gives a preview of 2:14–27, with 'faith' (2:1, 14) and 'doing right' (2:8, 19).[3]

*Favouritism forbidden*

**2** My brothers and sisters, believers in our glorious Lord Jesus Christ must not show favouritism. **2** Suppose a man comes into your meeting wearing a gold ring and fine clothes, and a poor man in filthy old clothes also comes in. **3** If you show special attention to the man wearing fine clothes and say, 'Here's a good seat for you,' but say to the poor man, 'You stand there'

1 James 2:1–13 has parallels with 1:1–27 that do not occur elsewhere: *diakrinō* in both 1:6 and 2:4 (NIV: 'doubt' and 'discriminate', respectively), 'promised [to] those who love him' in 1:12 and 2:5, and the 'law that gives freedom' in 1:25 and 2:12. James 2:1–13 also shares elements with 2:14–26 that are not in 1:1–27. Both have an opening thesis (2:1, 14), hypothetical situation (2:2–4, 15–17), expansion of the thesis (2:5–13, 18–25) and a concluding axiom (2:12–13, 26).

2 Taylor, *Text-Linguistic*, 91.

3 See my explanation in *Eschatological Approval*, 135–6. Also Lorin L. Cranford, 'An Exposition of James 2', *Southwestern Journal of Theology* 29 (1986): 20.

or 'Sit on the floor by my feet,' **4** have
you not discriminated among yourselves and become judges with evil
thoughts?

**5** Listen, my dear brothers and
sisters: has not God chosen those
who are poor in the eyes of the world
to be rich in faith and to inherit the
kingdom he promised those who
love him? **6** But you have dishon-
oured the poor. Is it not the rich
who are exploiting you? Are they not
the ones who are dragging you into
court? **7** Are they not the ones who
are blaspheming the noble name of
him to whom you belong?

**8** If you really keep the royal law
found in Scripture, 'Love your neighbour as yourself,'[a] you are doing
right. **9** But if you show favouritism,
you sin and are convicted by the
law as law-breakers. **10** For whoever
keeps the whole law and yet stumbles at just one point is guilty of
breaking all of it. **11** For he who said,
'You shall not commit adultery,'[b]
also said, 'You shall not murder.'[c] If
you do not commit adultery but do
commit murder, you have become a
law-breaker.

**12** Speak and act as those who are
going to be judged by the law that
gives freedom, **13** because judgment
without mercy will be shown to
anyone who has not been merciful.
Mercy triumphs over judgment.

---

**a** 8 Lev. 19:18
**b** 11 Exodus 20:14; Deut. 5:18
**c** 11 Exodus 20:13; Deut. 5:17

## 1. *Thesis statement • James 2:1*

James starts 2:1–13 with a thesis statement that his readers, who are Christ-followers, should not show favouritism. He gives three reasons to support this declaration: (a) do not judge by appearances, (b) God favours the poor, and (c) one must obey the whole law. As we will see, each of these reasons is associated with judgment.

## *2. Do not favour the rich • James 2:2–4*

As discussed above, James begins with the specific principle: avoiding favouritism to the rich. This leads to a more general exhortation to obey the law of God in expectation of judgment.

The social dimension of patronage was prevalent in the ancient Graeco–Roman world, to the point that Seneca called it 'the chief bond of human society'.[4] A person of a lower social class would often seek help for goods and services from someone more influential. If the figure of higher status granted the request, the two parties would enter a patron–client relationship. Patron–client relationships were characterised by inequality: the client was subordinate to the patron. The patron would then seek reciprocation from clients later.[5] For example, clients would reciprocate past favours by speaking well of a patron who was eyeing a political office. A patron–client relationship would usually be lifelong, and even passed to later generations.[6]

James's marginalised hearers, with limited access to goods and services, would likely desire to treat an influential figure well because of the principle of reciprocity. For the modern reader accustomed to gifts 'with no strings attached', the principle of reciprocity might induce discomfort. But a sense of reciprocal duty is commonplace in many cultures today, especially those influenced by Confucianism.[7] However, James urges his hearers

4 *On Benefits* 1.4.2. See Seneca the Younger, *De Beneficiis*, trans. John W. Basore (Cambridge, MA: Harvard University Press, 1935), 19.

5 For patronage and reciprocity, both ancient and modern, see Jayson Georges and Mark D. Baker, *Ministering in Honor-Shame Cultures: Biblical Foundations and Practical Essentials* (Downers Grove: IVP Academic, 2016), 46–52.

6 See David A. deSilva, *Honor, Patronage, Kinship, and Purity: Unlocking New Testament Culture* (Second Edition; Downers Grove: IVP Academic, 2022), 125–75.

7 Also see Eng, 'Asian Reflections on James', 256–7.

to refrain from giving unequal treatment, for this makes them guilty of breaking God's law.

The disdaining of favouritism was a central tenet of Israel. While the surrounding nations held those of higher status to be more valuable than those of lower status, the Old Testament urged the people to reflect the character of God and not to show favouritism. In Deuteronomy 10:17–19, we see the Lord defending and loving those of lower status: the fatherless, the widow, and the foreigner. The people were called to match God's character and care for the lowly.[8] In the New Testament as well, God is described as not having favouritism (see, for example, Acts 10:34; Romans 2:11; Colossians 3:25).Since those in the diaspora are themselves foreigners, James echoes the Old Testament formula, omitting 'foreigners'. He calls for them to care for the other marginalised groups.

The command comes with a hypothetical scenario in James 2:2–3. Two men enter their 'meeting', which is probably a synagogue.[9] Diaspora synagogues were prevalent; examples are seen in Acts 13:5; 14:1; 19:8. Synagogues were where diaspora Jews could gather for prayer, community and listening to the Scriptures.[10]

For these diaspora Jews far from Jerusalem, the synagogue offered a bastion for retaining their heritage. In the same way, modern diasporas of many ethnicities, after voluntary or forced migration, gather with others from their culture to maintain their identity.

Whether diaspora synagogues met in standalone buildings or

8 For more on God's character in the context of patronal relationships, see Jerry Hwang, *Contextualization and the Old Testament: Between Asian and Western Perspectives* (Carlisle, Cumbria: Langham Global Library, 2022), 105–10.

9 'Meeting' is *synagōgē*, occurring fifty-six times in the New Testament. In the other fifty-five instances, the NIV renders or considers it a 'synagogue'. The usage of *synagōgē* is significant, since James is aware of the word translated as 'church' (*ekklēsia*, 5:14). In the earliest days of the church, Christ-followers met in synagogues.

10 For more on diaspora synagogues, see deSilva, 'Diaspora', 278–81.

the home of a host, these local communities often depended on the generosity of a patron. For example, the Theodotus inscription from a synagogue dated to the first century describes a philanthropic donation: 'Theodotus . . . built the synagogue for reading the law and teaching the commandments.' Those who contributed funds to a synagogue were often esteemed with inscriptions and honorific titles.[11]

In the hypothetical scenario, a man wearing fine clothes and a gold ring enters the synagogue. For the underprivileged hearers of James, the presence of a prominent figure presents an opportunity. The man may be already an esteemed benefactor of the synagogue. By showing favour to him, the hearers could be reciprocating past generosity. However, it is also possible that the wealthy man is entering for the first time. If so, folks would treat him well, probably with anticipation that he would grant them a future favour in return. There is a *quid pro quo* dynamic occurring here.

Many modern cultures, especially those with roots in the Global East, value gift-giving and services from those with financial means and influence. In such collectivistic cultures, high-status individuals are expected to help the less fortunate. The lower-class beneficiaries then reciprocate, often by giving public esteem to the generous person.[12] In patronage-based societies, giving gifts establishes a lasting relationship. Likewise, gifts in the ancient world were not regarded as payment, but as an invitation into a mutual social bond. John Barclay writes that an ancient gift is 'filled with sentiment because it invites a personal, enduring, and reciprocal relationship'.[13]

---

11 Hubbard, *Christianity in the Greco-Roman World*, 132.

12 For a discussion of collectivistic cultures and ancient patronage, see E. Randolph Richards and Richard James, *Misreading Scripture with Individualist Eyes: Patronage, Honor, and Shame in the Biblical World* (Downers Grove: IVP Academic, 2020), 64–81.

13 John M. G. Barclay, *Paul and the Gift* (Grand Rapids: Eerdmans, 2015), 31.

The hypothetical scenario also includes 'a poor man in filthy old clothes' coming into the synagogue. The contrast between the two men is clear in their appearances: their clothing indicates their social rank. For example, in Roman culture, senators were known for their *toga pura*. Equestrians, of the second order, were known for wearing a gold ring.[14] The filthy clothes of the second man may indicate that he owns no clothes other than his labouring attire.

In the scenario, the hearers of James give an esteemed seat to the rich man and a lesser place to the poor man. One recalls Luke 14:7–11, where Jesus urges his hearers not to take the place of honour at a feast. Here in James, offering a good seat to the rich man is showing favouritism.

No culture is immune from discrimination in favour of the rich. Worldwide, from the British class system to the Indian caste system, those who are more fortunate are given preferential treatment. The poor, on the other hand, are left at the margins. An African proverb says, 'Thin cows are not licked by their friends.' They are 'thin' because they cannot offer any contribution to others – they are ignored.[15]

As we will see in James 2:5–7, showing favouritism to the rich while marginalising the poor is a violation of God's ways. Again, James echoes the sayings of Jesus:

> When you give a luncheon or dinner, do not invite your friends, your brothers or sisters, your relatives, or your rich neighbours; if you do, they may invite you back and so you will be repaid. But when you give a banquet, invite the poor, the crippled, the lame, the blind, and

14 Ingeborg Mongstad-Kvammen, *Toward a Postcolonial Reading of the Epistle of James: James 2:1–13 in its Roman Imperial Context* (Leiden: Brill, 2013), 100.

15 Tokunboh Adeyemo, ed. *Africa Bible Commentary* (Grand Rapids: Zondervan, 2006), 1538.

> you will be blessed. Although they cannot repay you, you will be repaid at the resurrection of the righteous. (Luke 14:12–14)

Today, favouritism can occur within our church communities. Suppose during a Sunday service you recognise an executive of a corporation that can offer your university-aged daughter an internship. Would you give preferential attention to the high-powered executive rather than to the teenage mother who slipped into the back of the sanctuary? Are we willing to set our selfish desires aside and align with the disadvantaged?

Showing favouritism follows the ways of the world, which James teaches his hearers to avoid (1:27; 4:4). He condemns favouritism, asking a rhetorical question in 2:4, 'Have you not discriminated among yourselves and become judges with evil thoughts?' Note that the term translated as 'discriminated' is used for 'doubt' in 1:6.[16] It is in the same word family as 'judge', which appears later in 2:4. As stated earlier, every usage of 'judge' or 'judging' in James where people are the subject is condemned. The 'evil thoughts' probably refer to the selfish desires that motivate preferential treatment to influential people. If followers of Christ show favouritism, we are no better than evil judges (see Luke 18:6) in the courts (James 2:7) who give advantage to the rich.

Indeed, God is the rightful judge. While people look at the outward appearance, God looks at the heart (see 1 Samuel 16:7). The hearers of James are not to usurp God's role as judge. God will be the one to judge when the end comes.

16 See the commentary at 1:6.

## *3. God favours the poor and opposes the rich • James 2:5–7*

James continues his support for 2:1, discussing the contrast between the poor and the rich. He poses several rhetorical questions, each implying a 'yes' answer. Together, they convey the cumulative message that God favours the poor and not the rich.

The first question points to a wider principle: in God's economy, the poor man should be honoured. Previously, James has affirmed the 'believers in humble circumstances' (1:8) and declared that God desires the hearers to care for the orphans and widows (1:27).

In discussing God's kindness towards the poor, James reminds his hearers of God's prior choice (2:5). Much like the birthing and firstfruits imagery in 1:18, God has called the weak and the lowly to be in his community (see 1 Corinthians 1:26–9). James declares that God has chosen the 'poor in the eyes of the world'.[17]

James's declaration does not mean that God has *only* chosen poor people and that the wealthy are excluded. However, there is a correlation between the poor and God's faithful people in biblical literature (for example, Psalm 9:18; 85:1; Isaiah 3:15; Luke 6:20). The early church largely consisted of those with limited material resources.[18]

Also, note that James does not refer to all the poor indiscriminately. He states that they can expect a future inheritance that is promised to 'those who love him'. This is a key qualifier: there is a reward for the poor who love God.

---

17 'In the eyes' does not occur in the Greek text, but it fits the context, especially with two men judged by their appearances. For a different interpretation, that the 'world' merely refers to physical location rather than status, see Pedrito U. Maynard-Reid, *Poverty and Wealth in James* (Maryknoll, NY: Orbis, 1987), 62.

18 Thomas D. Hanks calls the church 'the brotherhood of the poor' in *God So Loved the Third World*, trans. James C. Dekker (Eugene: Wipf and Stock, 2000), 46.

What exactly will the God-loving poor receive? First, James mentions being 'rich in faith',[19] which refers to God's standards of wealth. Much like Jesus calls his disciples to have treasure in heaven (see Matthew 6:20) and to be rich towards God (Luke 12:21). The chosen poor will have wealth 'by God's standards'.[20]

Modern marginalised peoples, like the hearers of James, would be tempted to envy the riches of those of higher classes. It is in these societies that the lies of the Prosperity Gospel – the messages that God offers health and wealth to the faithful – are most prevalent. But rather than put their hope in large mansions, expensive cars or social influence, James affirms God's standards of wealth.

Second, James indicates that the poor will also inherit the kingdom. By identifying the poor as the heirs, James acknowledges their identity or status in the eyes of God. While they are disadvantaged and living in disgrace, God honours the poor who love him with an esteemed status: they are *heirs*.

It is heirs who receive an inheritance, a future reward. The biblical image of inheritance describes an eternal reward for the righteous (Psalm 37:9, 29; Isaiah 60:21; 61:7). The most prominent parallel to James 2:5 is Matthew 25:34, where Jesus describes an inherited kingdom set in eternity for those who care for the poor. 'Inheritance' reminds these diaspora hearers of God's promises that the people would inherit the land (Exodus 15:17; Deuteronomy 8:1). Since they are outside the land and reminded of the Exile, this hope resonates deeply.

What is the kingdom to which James refers? God's kingdom is a prominent biblical theme, especially in the teachings of Jesus.

19 This phrase has three possible explanations: (a) having an abundance of faith, (b) becoming wealthy by having faith, or (c) being rich in the sphere of faith. Of the three, option (c) fits best. It creates a parallel between the world and the sphere of faith, where the poor will be rich in the latter. Also, being rich in the sphere of faith echoes Jesus's sayings about treasure in heaven.

20 Ropes, *St. James*, 194.

His reign is described as everlasting (see Psalm 146:10; Jeremiah 10:10; Daniel 7:14). In the teachings of Jesus, 'kingdom of God' occurs repeatedly, referring to (a) God's dynamic ruling activity in the present (Matthew 12:28; Luke 13:18–19), and (b) God's reign over the world in the future (Matthew 5:20; Mark 9:1; Luke 22:16).[21] The second meaning fits best with James 2:5: while disadvantaged by worldly systems, the poor can look forward to God's rule, where they will receive an inheritance.

The sayings of Jesus also associate 'inheriting the kingdom' with 'eternal life'. There appears to be a significant overlap between these two concepts (see Matthew 19:29; Mark 10:30; Luke 18:29–30). Jesus teaches that the judge will invite the righteous to 'take your inheritance' and have 'eternal life' (25:34, 46). Thus, this inheritance is intimately connected to the favourable eternal state that the righteous receive.

The parallel between James 2:5 and the epistle's thesis statement in 1:12 gives further support to identifying the kingdom as the favourable eternal state. Both sayings repeat the same phrase:

| | | |
|---|---|---|
| 1:12 | receive the crown of life | promised to those who love him |
| 2:5 | inherit the kingdom | promised those who love him |

Again, the heirs of the kingdom are those who love God, which recalls the *Shema*, the call to love God 'with all your heart and with all your soul and with all your strength' (Deuteronomy 6:5). Despite their stigma of being far from the land, the diaspora hearers can still be included in the people who inherit God's earthly reign. This is consistent with the epistle's thesis statement (1:12). If they remain faithful in loving God, they will be rich in faith and receive a favourable verdict at the end.

21 For the two meanings of *the kingdom of God*, see Norman Perrin, *The Kingdom of God in the Teaching of Jesus*, NTL (London: SCM, 1963), 160–85.

James 2:6a returns the hearers to the hypothetical scenario in 2:2–4. If the hearers practise the worldly ways of favouritism, they are dishonouring the very people that God honours. James urges his hearers to associate with the poor rather than the rich.

The next questions in James 2:6b–7 contrast the rich with the poor who love God, adding more justification to the declaration in James 2:1. James presents three accusations of the rich: they (a) exploit the hearers of the epistle, (b) drag them into court, and (c) blaspheme 'the noble name' to whom they belong.

First, the rich oppress the poor to their advantage.[22] James gives an example of exploitation at the end of 2:6 – they are dragging them into court. The rich probably use their influence to receive favourable verdicts in the local courts. Whether the disputes are about taxes or unfair wages (see 5:4), the rich can abuse their power.[23] In this way, James attributes poverty to the rich's wickedness, which he will also do in 5:4–6.[24] We can see this oppression in modern societies, too: the rich have allies in high places and can hire the best legal assistance.

Indeed, human courts are often influenced by favouritism. The Old Testament describes human judges that show favouritism (see Deuteronomy 1:17; Leviticus 19:15), but God does not (Deuteronomy 10:17).[25] Likewise, the judges in the courts in James 2:7 show favour to the rich, perhaps so they themselves can receive reciprocation later. Again, we see James repeat the motif that human judging is corrupt.

In James 2:7, the rich are also 'blaspheming the noble name of him to whom [they] belong'. James uses 'name' elsewhere (5:10,

---

22 See the verb for 'exploit' in Hosea 12:7 and Ezekiel 18:12.

23 Sophie S. Laws, *A Commentary on the Epistle of James* (London: Black, 1980), 105; Moo, *The Letter of James*, 139–40.

24 Hanks states that James sees oppression as the *basic reason* for poverty. See Hanks, *God So Loved the Third World*, 46.

25 See the commentary at 2:1. The Hebrew for favouritism is *nāśā᾽pānîm*, associated with the *face*.

14), and it probably refers to the name of Christ, to whom the hearers of James belong (see 2:1).[26] They may or may not be called 'Christians', but they are associated with Christ's name.[27] Christ's name is the highest (see Philippians 2:9–11), and blaspheming is a violation against God. The rich are blaspheming the Lord, either together with or through their exploitative actions.

## *4. One must obey the whole law • James 2:8–13*

James gives the third justification for his forbidding favouritism (2:1) in 2:8–11. He calls his hearers to adhere to the law – not just part of the law – the *whole law*. Since favouritism violates the teaching of God, practising favouritism makes one guilty of breaking the whole law. Christ-followers should not be picking and choosing which parts of God's character to imitate.

James calls the law 'royal', a designation that points to a king. This can refer to the Old Testament designation of Yahweh as the King (Psalm 95:3; Jeremiah 10:10), or to Christ (Hebrews 1:8; Matthew 25:34). Either sense can fit since the Torah's prescribed treatment of others is summed up in the love command (Leviticus 19:18), which is affirmed by Jesus (Luke 10:25–37). If the hearers of James love their neighbours, they reflect the good name and 'are doing right'.[28]

The Torah states that one must not show partiality, but treat people fairly (Leviticus 19:15; Deuteronomy 16:19). In 2:9, James goes beyond stating that favouritism breaks the law; favouritism gives them the *identity* of law-breakers. This act of being *convicted*

26 'Name' could allude to Israel being called by the name of God (see 2 Chronicles 7:14; Daniel 9:19).

27 'Noble' (*kalos*) contrasts the 'good' (*kalōs*) seat in 2:3. James makes it clear: what matters is not the worldly esteem of the good seat, but the good *name*.

28 There is a connection between 'right' (*kalōs*) doing and the 'good' (*kalos*) name in 2:7.

communicates God's judgment. They have willingly transgressed the law and are labelled as violators.[29]

James 2:10–11 gives support for the declaration in 2:9. Here, James discusses the law's unified nature: one must keep the *whole* law, not just parts of it. This all-or-nothing view is consistent with his description of the law as *perfect* in 1:25 and the idea of purity in 1:27. The concept of the law's unity is found elsewhere in the New Testament, in the teachings of Jesus (Matthew 5:18–19) and Paul (Galatians 5:3).

The shift from 'you' to 'whoever' in James 2:10 indicates that this is a proverbial truth. Forbidding favouritism is one part of the law, and breaking any part makes one guilty of being a law-breaker. For these diaspora hearers, the word 'stumbles' (also see 3:2) may evoke the figurative usage of *walking* in biblical literature, referring to living by God's teaching (for example, Deuteronomy 5:33; Joshua 22:5; Psalm 1:1; 1 John 1:7).

James gives an example of inconsistent keeping of the law with two teachings from the Ten Commandments. The one described as 'he who said' is God, who gave the law to Moses. Note the relational element in James's teaching. The source of the law is critical here: the two commands come from the same God and cannot be divided. It is God, the only Lawgiver and Judge (4:12), who spoke the law.[30] Followers of Christ should not be selective about which parts of God's character they adhere to.

The appeal to 'you shall not murder' is fitting here. Oppression of the poor and failure to love one's neighbour was frequently associated with murder in biblical literature (see Jeremiah 7:6; Amos 8:4; 1 John 3:15; possibly James 5:6).[31] Notably, James accuses his hearers of murder in 4:2 and calls them adulteresses

29 See Blomberg and Kamell, *James*, 117.

30 Johnson, *Letter of James*, 232.

31 See Davids, *Epistle of James*, 117.

in 4:4.[32] Following one law but not the other makes someone a law-breaker.

To be sure, James is not stating that all transgressions are equal. Jesus declares certain matters of the law more important (Matthew 23:23). We prefer someone to tell 'tell a "white lie" rather than initiate a nuclear holocaust'.[33] However, James's point is that favouritism to the rich violates the law, and any violation makes one guilty of being a law-breaker. If they pick and choose whom they show favour to, they are also picking and choosing which commandments to obey.

James has given three justifications for his forbidding of favouritism: (a) one is not to judge by appearances, (b) God favours the poor, and (c) a Christ-follower should imitate all of God's character. Each of these points to God as the judge, as human judges are condemned. In the next subsection, which serves as the opening to the main portion of the epistle's body, James appeals to end-time judgment, which is consistent with the repeating motif and thesis of the epistle.

In James 2:12–13, James sums up this subsection by giving a wider exhortation and offering a preview of the main body of James. As discussed above, James 2:12–13 forms an often-overlooked *inclusio* with 4:11–12, clustering terms for *judging*, *law* and *doing*. Also, both passages describe the importance of speech ethics and appeal to how one treats a neighbour. As 2:1–13 acts as a transition to the main body, 2:12–13 offers a 'hinge' that previews the large movements of 2:14–26; 3:1–12, 13–18 and 4:1–10.

James 2:12–13 has three parts: (a) an exhortation, (b) its reasoning, and (c) a pithy, timeless statement. In the first part (2:12), James urges his hearers to 'speak and act' in expectation

---

32 The Greek is feminine plural. A full explanation will be given at the commentary for 4:4.

33 Blomberg and Kamell, *James*, 119.

of judgment. The interplay between speaking and acting is a key theme in the epistle (for example, see 1:19–25; 2:14–16; 4:11). Consistency between speaking, acting and the law is an indicator of commitment to God. As stated in 1:25, the law 'gives freedom'. This freedom is not for rebellion against God, but for submitting to God and producing righteousness, leading to eternal life.

In the second part of these two verses, James 2:13a, James gives justification for the exhortation in 2:12. He writes that 'judgment without mercy will be shown to anyone who has not been merciful'. God is described as merciful (for example, Exodus 34:6; Psalm 145:9; Daniel 9:9), and he commands his people to show mercy (Micah 6:6–8; Luke 6:36). Jesus tells a parable about a master who condemned his servant who did not show mercy to a fellow servant (Matthew 18:32–4).

We must acknowledge that God's mercy does not contradict justice, since the Lord condemns guilt (see James 2:10).[34] Rather, mercy reflects justice as defined by God in the law. The people are called to show mercy, caring for the widow and the fatherless (Zechariah 7:9–10; see also Exodus 22:22; Deuteronomy 24:17). Jesus teaches us to show mercy to others just like we have been shown mercy by God.[35] The hypothetical scenario in James 2:2–3 shows an example of someone who has not been merciful. Such acts will receive judgment without mercy.

The third part of James 2:12–13 ends this subsection with a pithy, timeless statement: 'Mercy triumphs over judgment' (2:13b). This statement can be difficult to interpret, but we can be guided by its context. Neither 'mercy' nor 'judgment' are newly stated concepts. This judgment is from God; it is condemnation of evil (see 2:12). While mercy is an attribute of God, the passage has been discussing the mercy of people. Mercy in 2:13b, then, is

34 Also see Spencer, *A Commentary on James*, 138.

35 For example, see Matthew 5:7; 6:12, 14–15; 18:21–35. Blomberg and Kamell, *James*, 123.

most likely human mercy. Showing mercy to others demonstrates our love for God (1:12; 2:5) and our devotion to the 'royal law' (2:8). Since followers of Christ are united with him in his death and resurrection (Romans 6:5), his perfect adherence to the law becomes the basis for our vindication.[36] Thus, the saying can be restated this way: Followers of Christ who show mercy now can triumph; they will not be condemned in the end.

36 Moo, *The Letter of James*, 151.

# 6

# Faith and Deeds

## JAMES 2:14–26

After the 'bridge passage' of James 2:1–13, this section on faith and deeds in 2:14–26 marks the beginning of the epistle's main body.[1] This section is held together by the repeated interaction between 'faith' and 'deeds'. Further reinforcing its coherence, the beginning (2:14), middle (2:20) and end (2:26) of the passage repeat the concept that faith without deeds is worthless.

To be sure, James 2:14–26 has connections with the content before it. Like 2:1–13, it begins with a stated thesis (2:14), a hypothetical situation (2:15–17), an expansion of the thesis (2:18–25) and a pithy concluding statement (2:26). Like 2:1–13, it presents the topic of *having faith*. It also presents an exhortation with the phrase 'doing right' (rendered 'Good!' in the NIV at 2:19; see 2:8). Also, 2:14–16 continues the theme of wealth and the poor (1:27; 2:2–8) as a way of illuminating a wider principle.

Much of the discussion about this passage focuses on how it appears to conflict with Paul's teaching on faith, works and justification (especially in Romans and Galatians). While this commentary will discuss that topic, we will concentrate on the message that James has for his hearers. At the end of this discussion, we will address how it relates to Paul's teaching.

*Faith and deeds*

**14**What good is it, my brothers and sisters, if someone claims to have faith but has no deeds? Can

1 The body comprises of 2:14–4:12.

such faith save them? **15** Suppose a
brother or a sister is without clothes
and daily food. **16** If one of you says
to them, 'Go in peace; keep warm
and well fed,' but does nothing about
their physical needs, what good is
it? **17** In the same way, faith by itself,
if it is not accompanied by action,
is dead.

**18** But someone will say, 'You have
faith; I have deeds.'

Show me your faith without deeds,
and I will show you my faith by my
deeds. **19** You believe that there is
one God. Good! Even the demons
believe that – and shudder.

**20** You foolish person, do you want
evidence that faith without deeds is
useless[d]? **21** Was not our father Abraham considered righteous for what he
did when he offered his son Isaac on
the altar? **22** You see that his faith and
his actions were working together,
and his faith was made complete by
what he did. **23** And the scripture was
fulfilled that says, 'Abraham believed
God, and it was credited to him as
righteousness,'[e] and he was called
God's friend. **24** You see that a person
is considered righteous by what they
do and not by faith alone.

**25** In the same way, was not even
Rahab the prostitute considered
righteous for what she did when she
gave lodging to the spies and sent
them off in a different direction?
**26** As the body without the spirit is
dead, so faith without deeds is dead.

**d** 20 Some early manuscripts *dead*
**e** 23 Gen. 15:6

## 1. *Thesis statement • James 2:14*

Repeating the motif of speech ethics, James opens with a rhetorical question about a 'claim'.[2] Like other writers who used rhetorical dialogue,[3] James starts by refuting a proposition, asking, 'What good is it?' The rhetorical question anticipates a negative reply: 'It is no good at all!'

The rhetorical question continues the interplay between

2 The term rendered 'claims' in the NIV is the same as 'speak' elsewhere.

3 For example, see 1 Corinthians 15:32 and Sirach 20:30.

'speaking' and 'doing' in the epistle. While a person claims to have faith, there are no deeds consistent with that faith. James has already used the word 'faith' repeatedly (1:3, 6; 2:1, 5), where it describes one's trusting commitment to Christ. James affirms a commitment that is unwavering (1:6–8) and paired with a commitment to fulfilling the law (1:22–5; 2:1).

The term for 'deeds' does occur elsewhere in James (1:4, 25; 3:13), but there are twelve instances in 2:14–26. It is sometimes rendered as 'works' in other English translations, which would be consistent with the NIV in Romans 3:20 and Galatians 2:16. However, in the context of James 2:14, the NIV's rendering of 'deeds' is helpful because it describes the good deeds of mercy (2:15–16). Speaking or claiming to have faith should not be its only expression; it should be expressed in good deeds.[4]

James asks a second rhetorical question in 2:14: 'Can such faith save them?' When referring to 'such faith', it is the type that has no good deeds. Therefore, James considers two kinds of faith: one accompanied by good deeds, and one that is not. The implied answer to this second question is also negative: such faith has no value; it cannot save them.

Given the repeated appeals to eschatological judgment in James, 'save' refers to eternal life, to eschatological salvation. James states that a faith that is expressed verbally but without action is not salvific. This is corroborated by the earlier use of the same term in 1:21, which refers to the salvation of souls, and the usage of it outside James in the New Testament.[5] In other words, when judgment comes, which sort of faith will save? James makes it clear: the sort of faith that is accompanied by good deeds.

---

4 Ralph P. Martin, *James* (Waco, TX: Word, 1988), 81; Davids, *Epistle of James*, 121.TX: Word, 1988

5 The term for 'save' is used thirty times in New Testament epistles outside James, with twenty-nine of them referring to eschatological salvation. See Moo, *The Letter of James*, 156–7.

## 2. *Hypothetical scenario: a needy brother or sister • James 2:15–17*

James illustrates the futility of a spoken faith devoid of good deeds. In accordance with his repeated emphasis on the poor and lowly (1:9, 27; 2:2–7), he gives an example of a brother or sister lacking in clothes and food. The inclusion of 'sister' here shows that the scenario is widely encompassing.[6]

The appeal to a hypothetical scenario about a poor person is more poignant to those in the modern Global East and South, where poverty is prevalent and visible. Even with the affluence of the West, there are needy people everywhere. One can look at those experiencing homelessness, at refugees or at those on government assistance to find needy people in our communities.

One should not take the specificity of 'a brother or sister' in the hypothetical scenario to mean that followers of Christ should care for those within the community of faith to the exclusion of outsiders. The previous hypothetical scenario (James 2:2–4) describes two men – one rich and one poor – coming 'into' the meeting from the outside. Also, James declares favour on those in humble circumstances in James 1:9.

Here, the author uses the hypothetical scenario to describe the pointless nature of speaking a wish for welfare without doing anything for someone's needs. Without action, the saying, 'Keep warm and well fed,' has no value. It is much like the modern phenomenon of 'slacktivism', or merely agreeing with a cause through posting on social media without acting. A recent advertising campaign for a humanitarian relief organisation used the slogan 'Liking Isn't Helping', showing the futility of social media lip service without doing anything to help those in need.[7]

---

6 It may also recall the needy widows in 1:27.

7 Thanks to Andrew Eddy for this illustration.

In 2:17, James restates the thesis of 2:14 in different words: 'In the same way, faith by itself, if it is not accompanied by action, is dead.' Just like wishing a needy person well without meeting their needs is useless, simply stating that one has faith is useless without the verification of action. Indeed, Jesus spoke about the futility of verbal assent without accompanying deeds (Luke 6:46): 'Why do you call me, "Lord, Lord," and not do what I say?'

## *3. Imaginary debate • James 2:18–26*

James then provides more justification for his thesis that faith without accompanying deeds is useless. To persuade his hearers, he debates with an imaginary dialogue partner – an interlocutor – in the ancient diatribe style.[8]

It is unclear to which parties the pronouns 'you' and 'I' refer. On the one hand, the NIV's added quotation marks would make 'you' refer to James and 'I' to the interlocutor. On the other hand, one could punctuate as several short sentences: *But someone will speak. You have faith. I have deeds.* This would make 'you' refer to the interlocutor and the 'I' refer to James. The latter rendering would be more compatible with James's challenge at the end of 2:18. Ultimately, however one takes the pronouns, it remains clear that James refutes the claim that a faith devoid of accompanying deeds has salvific value.

In 2:19, James addresses his interlocutor: 'You believe that there is one God. Good!' The saying evokes the *Shema* (see the commentary at 1:12 and 1:19–25), where Moses declared to Israel: 'The LORD our God, the LORD is one' (Deuteronomy 6:4). This saying embodies part of Israel's unique identity: their monotheism. There is only one God: the God of Abraham, Isaac and Jacob.

8 The general nature of this letter suggests that the interlocutor is imaginary.

But James insists that assent to the proposition of one God is inadequate. In a jarring declaration, he states, 'Even the demons believe that – and shudder.' A faith with value must go beyond that of the demons. After all, the demons hold to monotheism – they are 'neither atheists nor agnostics', says Warren Wiersbe.[9] However, this kind of faith does not save (see 2:14), since they do not have deeds.[10] With merely a declaration, one is no better than the demons.

In James 2:20, our author again states the thesis in 2:14, directing it towards his interlocutor: 'You foolish person, do you want evidence that faith without deeds is useless?' The adjective for 'foolish' appears to carry the sense that the person is 'useless' or acting 'in vain'.[11] Ironically, just like deedless faith is useless, so is the *person* who claims to have such faith.

Walter Lewin is a retired professor of physics at the Massachusetts Institute of Technology. The video of his farewell lecture, 'For the Love of Physics', has been viewed more than 17 million times on YouTube.[12] In it, Lewin demonstrates the concept of the conservation of energy using a heavy ball hanging on a pendulum in the centre of the room. Standing against the wall, he places the ball on his chin and releases it to swing. He trusts that energy conservation would make the ball swing back, but not high enough to crush his face. By putting his life on the line, he demonstrates his belief in the

9 Warren W. Wiersbe, *Be Mature: Growing up in Christ* (Colorado Springs: David C. Cook, 2008), 86.

10 There is a minority view that 'shuddering' at God is itself a deed that demonstrates belief. This would bring even more disgrace to James's interlocutor. James's point remains: in order to be saving faith, it has to be of a different sort than the demons' belief.

11 See its usage in 1 Corinthians 15:14; 1 Thessalonians 2:1. The term often describes something empty (see Mark 12:3).

12 Walter Lewin, 'For the Love of Physics', YouTube, 16 May 2011.

principles he taught. In this way, he not only believes, but he puts his faith into action.

James then shows that faith must be paired with deeds through two Old Testament examples: Abraham (2:21–3) and Rahab (2:25). First, James appeals to Genesis 22, where Abraham's willingness to offer up his son shows that he fears God (Genesis 22:12). The account begins in Genesis 22:1 with the words, 'God tested Abraham.'[13] The notion of a divine evaluator is consistent with James's motif of God as the judge. This testing of one's actions, then, is the prerequisite for the key term found in James 2:21 – 'considered righteous', or in other translations, 'justified'.

The nineteenth-century evangelist D. L. Moody stated that 'every Bible should be bound in shoe leather'.[14] One must not just know the faith, but also walk in it. The co-working of Abraham's faith and actions produced the favourable result. Also, the ongoing nature of the co-working shows that Abraham's faith was not alone; it was shown to be true by demonstration.

Furthermore, James states that their esteemed ancestor's faith 'was made complete by what he did' (2:22). There is a relationship characterised by mutuality. First, faith directs the actions, and in turn, actions make faith complete. In other words, faith is brought to maturity (see the commentary at 1:4) by deeds. One cannot exist without the other.

One may wonder if James is stating that good deeds offer some sort of merit for salvation. But James has stated earlier (2:14) that one is saved by *faith* – that is, a particular sort of faith. John Calvin is credited with the saying, 'It is . . . faith

---

13 In the LXX of Genesis 22, 'test' (*peirazō*) is the cognate of the nouns for 'trial' in James 1:2 and 1:12.

14 Wiersbe, *Be Mature*, 90.

alone that justifies, and yet the faith which justifies is not alone.'[15] Saving faith is not merely a mental exercise. It works in synergy with deeds as the righteous life matures. As we see next with the examples of Abraham and Rahab, saving faith shows itself through deeds.

James 2:23 then highlights two results of Abraham's co-working of faith and actions. First, the saying in Genesis 15:6 was fulfilled: Abraham believed God, and he was credited with righteousness. The two parts are distinct: his faith was expressed in Genesis 15, and his later deeds (Genesis 22) demonstrated that faith. The passive voice of 'it was credited' points to God's verdict on Abraham's faith.[16] The offering of Isaac was a deed of faith, but this does not preclude the other acts in Abraham's life – such as welcoming the three visitors or interceding for Sodom (see Genesis 18) – from also contributing to the synergy with faith.

The second result of Abraham's co-working faith and actions is that 'he was called God's friend' (see Isaiah 41:8; 2 Chronicles 20:7). Given the contrast with the faith of demons (James 2:19), this designation likely refers to allegiance or loyalty. Abraham's offering up of Isaac showed that he was loyal to God. The connotation of a friend with loyalty is found later in James 4:4 – one cannot be loyal to both the world and God. Continuing the pattern of presenting concepts in dichotomies, Abraham's faith showed his loyalty to God and no one else.

There is a likely connection between the term 'friend' and the ancient custom of patronage (see commentary at 2:2).[17] Because a client was subordinate to the patron, the term 'client' was considered degrading. Instead, a patron would often call his

---

15 John Calvin, 'Acts of the Council of Trent with the Antidote', in *John Calvin Tracts and Letters. Volume 3: Tracts, Part 3*, ed. Henry Beveridge (Edinburgh: Banner of Truth, 2009), 152.

16 Faith is not a 'principle of achievement'. See Martin, *James*, 94.

17 For a discussion of ancient friendship in relation to this passage, see Alicia J. Batten, *Friendship and Benefaction in James* (Dorset: Deo, 2010), 136–43.

client a 'friend' (*philos*).[18] Patronal relationships were defined by loyalty – one could never be a *philos* to two competing patrons (see James 4:4).[19]

For Abraham, 'friend' is likely an honorific title. Being a 'friend' of a powerful figure was a designation of esteem. In the LXX, a royal official is called a *philos* of the king (1 Chronicles 27:33; Esther 1:3; 2:18; 3:1; 6:9). When the Jewish leaders heckle Pilate at the trial of Jesus, they declare that if he releases the so-called King of the Jews, he is not a *philos* of Caesar (John 19:12). For Abraham, his obedient allegiance makes him worthy of being a 'friend' of God.

James 2:24 presents a timeless statement: 'A person is considered righteous by what they do and not by faith alone.' Often rendered as 'justified',[20] the connotation of this term (*dikaioutai*) with 'considered righteous' is found in the sayings of Jesus (see Luke 18:14). A person is proved righteous through righteous action.[21] Note that Abraham's deeds show him to have a relationship with God; he was God's friend. A person demonstrates one's relationship to another – including marriage, alliances and enemies (see James 4:4) – by what they do, and not by declaration alone. Likewise, one demonstrates right relationship with God through good deeds.

James 2:24 is a worthy summary of the argument. Like a person saying, 'Go in peace,' but not acting to help, or a demon acknowledging monotheism but not adhering to God, faith alone

18 Richard P. Saller, *Personal Patronage Under the Early Empire* (Cambridge: Cambridge University Press, 1982), 8–11.

19 I make the case that Jesus uses *philos* this way in John 15:13–15 in Daniel K. Eng, '"I Call You Friends": Jesus as Patron in John 15', *Themelios* 46, no. 1 (2021): 55–69.

20 See NRSV, KJV, ESV.

21 Also see Matthew 11:19 and Luke 7:35, where the NIV has 'proved right'. In the LXX, the same connotation is found, for example in Exodus 23:7; Isaiah 43:26; Micah 6:11.

is not enough. Abraham not only had faith, he also demonstrated it. Again, James appeals to an evaluation: the eschatological judgment.

James continues the argument with Rahab, whose account is primarily told in Joshua 2. In several ways, she is the antithesis of Abraham: a woman, not of Israel and – as James emphasises – a prostitute. Despite being different from the celebrated patriarch, the Canaanite 'harlot' is also considered righteous. What these two figures have in common is the point James is making: both are shown to be righteous by the same criterion: their deeds.

Rahab is not considered righteous by her lineage, gender or social reputation, but by her faith-actions. First, she trusted that the God of Israel is the Creator (Joshua 2:9–11). Second, she expressed her faith in God by assisting the spies and keeping them safe (Joshua 2:1–7, 15–21). She likely risked her life by misleading the messengers of the king of Jericho. Ultimately, Rahab receives honour; she is an ancestor of Christ (Matthew 1:5) and is upheld as an exemplar of faith (Hebrews 11:31).

We must recognise the order of the events as James presents them. Abraham and Rahab being 'considered righteous' is not a matter of conversion; he is not discussing the entry into a relationship with God. The evaluations of Abraham and Rahab come after their actions. Likewise, 'brothers and sisters' of James already have faith in Christ (see James 2:1). James is not discussing their conversion, but whether they have faith that co-works with action. Consistent with the epistle's thesis (1:12), James wants them to receive a 'divine declaration of righteousness that is in accord with the facts', as Dale Allison puts it.[22]

In James 2:26, the author again summarises with another timeless axiom (see 2:17 and 2:24). He likens the relationship between faith and deeds to that of the body and spirit. At first glance, the correspondence appears reversed: one might think

22 Allison, *James*, 483.

that deeds would go with the physical body while faith has a spiritual nature. But James is making an apt parallel. The body is 'an empty crafted pot', waiting to be filled.[23] Without some kind of vivifying spirit, a profession of faith is dead. Similarly, faith with no action to fill it has no life; without life-giving deeds, it is dead.

---

23 Spencer, *A Commentary on James*, 156.

# Excursus: Paul and James on Faith, Deeds and Justification

Martin Luther quipped that James has 'nothing of the nature of the gospel about it' and called it 'an epistle of straw',[1] an allusion to 1 Corinthians 3:12–13.[2] He further quipped that James 'is flatly against St. Paul and all the rest of Scripture in ascribing justification to works [2:24]'.[3] But do the teachings of both apostles actually contradict? Now that we have examined James's message on its own, we will address its relation to Paul's teaching. We will especially focus on the messages in Romans and Galatians, which are often brought into conversation with James 2:14–26.

First, we will compare how James and Paul use the term 'justified'. As discussed above, James refers to someone's verification or vindication after an action is done. In this way, the NIV's rendering of 'considered righteous' (James 2:21, 24, 25) is suitable. James is referring to the evaluation of someone after an action, as shown in the examples of Abraham and Rahab. In fact, Paul uses it this way as well, in Romans 3:4, a quotation of Psalm 51:4: 'That you may be proved right when you speak'.[4]

1 Martin Luther, 'Prefaces to the New Testament (1546)', in *Word and Sacrament I*, ed. E. Theodore Bachman, trans. Charles M. Jacobs (Philadelphia: Muhlenberg Press, 1960), 362.

2 Laws, *Epistle of James*, 1.

3 Martin Luther, 'Prefaces to the Epistles of St. James and St. Jude (1546)', in Bachman (ed.) and Jacobs (trans.), *Word and Sacrament I*, 396.

4 The ESV, NRSV and KJV all translate this as 'justified'.

However, Paul also uses the term 'justified' in a different way. He discusses it in the context of how a person *first* enters into a relationship with God – namely, conversion. In Romans 3:20–4:12 and Galatians 2:15–3:29, Paul describes how people are justified by faith. In both epistles, he declares that both Jews and Gentiles are 'justified', or brought into a right relationship with God, by the same criteria.[5] This usage of 'justified' largely diverges from that of James, Jesus and the LXX. Perhaps, then, one should wonder why Paul – not James – departs from convention.

While James discusses how an already-faithful person is expressing their faith, Paul discusses the dynamics surrounding one's entrance into relationship with Christ. James discusses the end – the evaluation of a life – while Paul discusses the beginning. If both were physicians, James would be the geriatrician while Paul would be the paediatrician.

Second, how do James and Paul define 'faith'? For both authors, the term is *pistis*. James, in 2:14–26, describes two sorts of faith: he writes, 'Can such faith save him?' The first sort of faith is not accompanied by action, the faith of the demons (2:19) – this faith is dead (2:17, 26). The second sort of faith is the type that does save: the faith of Abraham and Rahab. This saving faith is indeed accompanied by action – some specify it as *faithfulness*. This sort of faith will result in a favourable divine evaluation in the end.

In the appeal to demons in 2:19, James associates faith with adherence to the one God. Monotheism is a central tenet of Israel, described in the *Shema*.[6] Abraham and Rahab are appropriate

---

5 For an analysis of the nature of justification, see James B. Prothro, *Both Judge and Justifier: Biblical Legal Language and the Act of Justifying in Paul* (Tübingen: Mohr Siebeck, 2018).

6 For more, see Kim Huat Tan, 'James and the Shema', *Trinity Theological Journal* 15 (2007): 113–28.

examples because both are converts to adherence to Yahweh. Abraham is the original proselyte, being converted from the paganism of the Chaldeans. Rahab also was a proselyte, joining Israel (Joshua 2:11; 6:23).

Paul, however, associates faith with receiving the atoning sacrifice of Jesus Christ (Romans 3:25). Elsewhere, Paul writes that those with faith in Christ are justified, not by the works of the law (Galatians 2:16). Whether Paul uses 'faith' to refer to human activity (faith in Christ) or Christ's work (Christ's faithfulness), he clearly associates the follower of Christ with Christ's work.

Third, how do James and Paul define 'deeds' or 'works'? In both contexts, the term is *erga*. The term is a cognate of *ergonomic*, relating to work or activity. In James, the fifteen instances of the term (twelve in 2:14–26) are used only positively. It refers to the good deeds done by someone who is aligned with God and his word (see 1:25; 2:15–16).

Paul, on the other hand, uses the particular phrase 'works of the law' (*erga nomou*, see Romans 3:20, 28; Galatians 2:16). He uses this phrase negatively, referring to actions adhering to the Mosaic law, done to merit favour from God. To Paul, 'works of the law' are epitomised by circumcision. Paul was battling the false teaching that Gentiles had to undergo circumcision to be united with Christ (Galatians 2:1–16; 5:1–12; Romans 2:25–3:2; 4:9–12). He pits 'faith' (association with Christ) against 'works of the law', stating that one is justified by faith and not by works of the law (Galatians 2:16; Romans 3:28).

Ultimately, Paul and James would agree that people are saved by faith, not by meritorious action. They would also agree that a saving faith for a Christ-follower necessarily expresses itself in good deeds. However, in their different contexts, they were battling against different heresies. On the one hand, Paul was likely battling *legalism* – countering those who attempted to use the Mosaic law to gain and maintain status with God. Ultimately, whether or not Paul was battling legalism, this reliance on the law apart from Christ marginalises his work on the cross (see Galatians 2:21).

The controversy between Jews and Gentiles was a key part of the messages of Romans and Galatians. Paul was insisting that one did not have to follow the works of the law – become a Jew – to be a Christian. James, on the other hand, was battling against *antinomianism* – countering those who claim to have saving faith but using the claim as a licence for not doing good deeds.

Both the distinctions and the compatibility of the arguments of Paul and James are evident in how they appeal to the example of Abraham. Consider the timeline of these events of Abraham's life:

| | |
|---|---|
| Genesis 15:6 | 'Abram believed the LORD, and he credited it to him as righteousness.' |
| Genesis 17 | Abraham was circumcised. |
| Genesis 22 | God tested Abraham. |

Paul appeals to the example of Abraham by citing Genesis 15:6 in Romans 4:3. Here, he makes the case that Abraham was not 'justified' by 'works'. The example he uses for works is circumcision, a rite commanded by the Mosaic law. Paul states that Abraham was already considered righteous before he was circumcised (Romans 4:9–10). Significantly, circumcision is initiatory – it indicates the entry into the covenant with Yahweh. But, as Paul argues, circumcision was not the catalyst by which Abraham entered God's people, since he was already credited with righteousness earlier in his life. In Genesis 15:6, Abraham was justified, or entered into a relationship with God, by faith, not by his adherence to the law that did not yet exist.

Paul makes a similar argument regarding Abraham in Galatians. A key concern in Galatians is whether Gentile converts to Christianity should be required to receive circumcision and to practise the requirements of the Mosaic law. In his argument against the false teaching of the Judaisers (Galatians 2:14), Paul points out to the Galatians that they, like Abraham, were justified not by works of the law but through faith in Jesus Christ (Galatians 2:16–17; see also 3:11, 24; 5:4). Since Abraham was considered righteous before the law was given, those who have faith in Christ are children of Abraham (Galatians 3:6–7).

James, on the other hand, appeals to how Abraham's faith was vindicated. His argument, as we have discussed above, is that Abraham's faith co-worked with his obedience to show that it was a saving faith. In contrast to Paul, James is focused on Abraham's whole life.[7] The hearers of James understand that Abraham's deeds – particularly his obedient offering of Isaac – show him to be righteous.

Ultimately, an examination of the arguments used by James and Paul shows their teachings to be compatible. Both would agree that one is saved by faith, a particular type of faith that would show itself in good deeds. Later in Galatians, Paul states that what counts is 'faith expressing itself through love' (Galatians 5:6). He describes the crucifying of fleshly desires and the fruit of the Spirit: outward demonstrations of saving faith (Galatians 5:22–4). James's example of showing care to a needy brother or sister (James 2:15–16) is fitting with the declaration that the Lord desires mercy (Hosea 6:6; Matthew 9:13). It is by these outward demonstrations that one vindicates saving faith.

7 Chris Bruno, *Paul vs. James: What We've Been Missing in the Faith and Works Debate* (Chicago: Moody Publishers, 2019), 89.

# 7

# Taming the Tongue

## JAMES 3:1–12

Like in James 2:1–13, in 3:1–12 our author starts with a specific exhortation, then moves to a general concept. He opens in 3:1 with the command to be reluctant to become teachers, then proceeds to discuss the use of the tongue. The latter topic ends up being the focus of the section, with no further mention of teaching in particular.

After urging his hearers to be 'slow to speak' (James 1:19) and to rein their tongues (1:26), James gives two hypothetical scenarios in 2:3 and 2:16 which involve quotations of direct speech. The exhortation in 2:12, which is a preview of the body of the epistle, states that coming judgment should motivate righteous speech.[1] It is in 3:1–12 that the author gives the lengthiest discussion about the tongue in this epistle.

James opens with a warning against becoming a teacher (3:1–2). The content will expand to discuss the tongue in general: its disproportionate impact (3:3–6), the difficulty of keeping it under control (3:7–8) and a condemnation of using the tongue to both bless and to curse (3:9–12).

*Taming the tongue*

**3** Not many of you should become teachers, my fellow believers, because you know that we who teach will be judged more strictly. **2** We all stumble in many ways. Anyone who

1 For a study of the tongue in James, see William R. Baker, *Personal Speech-Ethics in the Epistle of James* (Tübingen: Mohr Siebeck, 1995).

is never at fault in what they say
is perfect, able to keep their whole
body in check.

**3** When we put bits into the mouths
of horses to make them obey us,
we can turn the whole animal. **4** Or
take ships as an example. Although
they are so large and are driven by
strong winds, they are steered by a
very small rudder wherever the pilot
wants to go. **5** Likewise, the tongue is
a small part of the body, but it makes
great boasts. Consider what a great
forest is set on fire by a small spark.
**6** The tongue also is a fire, a world
of evil among the parts of the body.
It corrupts the whole body, sets the
whole course of one's life on fire, and
is itself set on fire by hell.

**7** All kinds of animals, birds, reptiles
and sea creatures are being tamed
and have been tamed by mankind,
**8** but no human being can tame the
tongue. It is a restless evil, full of
deadly poison.

**9** With the tongue we praise our
Lord and Father, and with it we curse
human beings, who have been made
in God's likeness. **10** Out of the same
mouth come praise and cursing. My
brothers and sisters, this should not
be. **11** Can both fresh water and salt
water flow from the same spring?
**12** My brothers and sisters, can a
fig-tree bear olives, or a grapevine
bear figs? Neither can a salt spring
produce fresh water.

## *1. Opening command: not many should become teachers • James 3:1a*

Some propose that the admonition against becoming teachers may indicate a particular sort: teaching in the church. This would be consistent with the Jewish synagogue being a house of study, a *beth-hamidrash*, and the location of the hypothetical scenario in James 2:2. Teachers direct the affairs of the church, having leadership and authority.[2] However, narrowing the scope of teachers to those in the church would raise a certain irony: James is a teacher in the church, urging others not to do what

2 Martin, *James*, 104.

he does. Also, discouraging many from teaching in the church may appear incompatible with the New Testament's general posture of honouring and affirming the church's teachers (see, for example, 2 Timothy 2:2; Romans 12:7; Galatians 6:6).

A key to this exhortation is James's motif of socioeconomic disparity. As we have already seen, the poor and lowly are favoured in this epistle, while the rich are condemned. In the world of the hearers of James, those of lower social class would be motivated to gain more influence. The scenario in James 2:2–4 illustrates a temptation to show favouritism to the rich in order to receive reciprocal favours or status.[3] The hearers of James, being of lower class, would be tempted to seek esteem, possibly via the status of teacher. Jesus warned his disciples that they are not to be called 'Rabbi', but that they were all of the same status (Matthew 23:8). This sentiment would especially resonate in modern cultures where teachers are held in high regard. In Asia, for example, teachers are addressed as 'sir' or 'madam' and students often bow to them.[4]

As mentioned above, James includes himself in the category of teacher, moving from the second person ('you') to the first person ('we'). Despite himself being a teacher, he discourages his hearers from seeking the same role.

## *2. Two reasons to avoid becoming teachers • James 3:1b–2*

James justifies his discouragement to his hearers from aspiring to be teachers for two reasons. He is not exempt from these

---

3 I discuss socioeconomic disparity in James in Daniel K. Eng, 'The Letter of James', in *An Asian Introduction to the New Testament*, ed. Johnson Thomaskutty (Minneapolis: Fortress Press, 2022), 460–63.

4 Luke L. Cheung and Andrew B. Spurgeon, *James: A Pastoral and Contextual Commentary* (Carlisle: Langham Global Library, 2018), 65.

points, as he changes to the first-person 'we' to refer to those who teach.

First, those who teach 'will be judged more strictly'.[5] This continues the repeated motif of judgment in the epistle: the unstated judge is God, and James refers to future eschatological judgment. The stricter judgment on teachers is consistent with other biblical teaching, especially against false teachers. False prophets were condemned and to be put to death (Jeremiah 14:15; Ezekiel 22:28–31; Deuteronomy 18:20–22). Destruction is predicted for false teachers (Matthew 7:15–20; 2 Corinthians 11:13–15; 2 Peter 2:1–3; Revelation 19:20; 20:10).

Scripture also speaks about higher or lower standards of judgment. For example, Jesus taught that those who have more knowledge are held to a higher standard (see Luke 12:47–8). Indeed, James pronounces judgment on those who *know* the good but do not do it (James 4:17).

Author and spoken word artist Jackie Hill Perry, commenting on people seeking esteem, calls the role of teacher 'a dangerous occupation'. She advises, 'Don't pursue the position if you're unwilling to embrace the responsibility.' It is easier today to posture ourselves as Bible teachers than it was during the time of James. We can look outside the local church, where we can easily set up channels on social media and comment on the Scriptures.[6] For those who teach, James declares, there will be a stricter judgment.

Second, in James 3:2 the author discourages the pursuit of being a teacher by stating 'We all stumble in many ways.' While the scope of 'we all' could refer to humankind in general, it is more likely that it refers to him and his hearers (see 3:1).[7] Not only do they err, but they do so in many ways.

---

5 Woodenly, 'we will receive a greater judgment'. The term 'judgment' *(krima)* refers to a legal verdict.

6 Jackie Hill-Perry, 'The Incredible Power of Words', YouTube, 2021.

7 'We all' could refer to teachers in particular, but the context suggests that

James then states that a person who is 'perfect' does not stumble 'in what they say'. Teachers do a great deal of speaking, making this a natural transition for discussing the tongue. Jesus declared that all people will be held accountable for every empty word they speak (Matthew 12:36). Because they speak a lot, teachers must be especially prudent.

As James 1:4 indicates, being 'perfect' is the final goal of Christ-followers. A person who is 'perfect' can keep their entire body, not just their tongue, under control. The verb for 'keep in check' in 3:2 is the same as 'keep a tight rein' found in 1:26, also about the tongue. Hence James uses the imagery of a bridle on an animal, which will be expanded in the subsequent content.

Suspected criminals in police custody in the United States are reminded of their so-called Miranda rights: 'You have the right to remain silent. Anything you say can and will be used against you in a court of law.' Why are these rights valuable? Because we are responsible for the words we speak. Someone under arrest can choose their words carefully or remain quiet. James's teaching reminds the reader that we have the same choice.[8]

Careless words can often come out of our mouths. We can find it endearing when children blurt out their thoughts, but the mark of maturity is the ability to hold one's tongue. We know full well how prone we are to saying words that we would regret: either false or harmful words. It is a biblical virtue to keep control over one's words:

> Even fools are thought wise if they keep silent, and
> discerning if they hold their tongues.
> (Proverbs 17:28)

---

all the hearers addressed in 3:1 are in view. See Moo, *The Letter of James*, 187.

8 Courtney Doctor, *Steadfast: A Devotional Bible Study on the Book of James* (Deerfield, IL: The Gospel Coalition, 2019), 113.

## *3. The power of the tongue • James 3:3–6*

In James 3:3–6, our author justifies his assertion that the tongue is difficult to keep in check. While it is a small part of the body, the tongue has a disproportionately large impact. James gives three illustrations: a bit, a rudder and a spark.

The first illustration compares a small bit to a large animal, a horse. Continuing the imagery of a horse and bridle (see the commentary at 3:2a), James writes about putting bits into horses' mouths to control them. While a bit is small, it enables the rider of a horse to compel the much larger animal. James illustrates disproportionate power: a small bit controls a large animal, and a small tongue has great power.

The second illustration is similar to the first: a small rudder of a large ship. Here, James adds the 'strong winds' as another contrast to the small rudder. Despite the greatness of the vessel and the winds, having a rudder allows the pilot to control a large ship through violent storms because of this relatively small part.

James makes sure to use imagery from the world of his hearers. For them, a horse and a ship are two large items used for transportation. If he were to write in our modern day, perhaps he would discuss a steering wheel on a bus or the ailerons on an aeroplane.

The key to the first two illustrations is the *human* who controls the small item – the bit or the rudder. Likewise, the tongue has power, but it is in the hands of someone who must guide it and control it. As James stated earlier (1:26), a person devoted to the Lord must 'keep a tight rein' on their tongue. They must control their tongue, for it is a small part of the body with great power.

As with all illustrations, one should not take them too far. James is not teaching that the tongue controls a person's body like the rudder controls the ship. Rather, James is focusing on its relative size and disproportionate power, as he continues, 'Likewise, the tongue is a small part of the body, but it makes great boasts.'[9]

The boasting could be neutral, simply referring to the tongue's great ability. But James's other instances of boasting (see 3:14–16; 4:16–17), along with the content immediately after 3:5, favour this portrayal of boasting being negative. Indeed, the biblical concept of boasting is often negative, referring to arrogance in the face of God. For example, a very similar phrase is found in Psalm 12:3–4, where it is used in this negative sense:

> May the LORD silence all flattering lips
>   and every boastful tongue –
> those who say,
>   'By our tongues we will prevail;
>   our own lips will defend us – who is lord over us?'[10]

James 3:5b features a third illustration about the small tongue and its large impact: 'Consider what a great forest is set on fire by a small spark.'[11] This illustration differs from the first two. There is no figure controlling the small item, and this time the impact is destructive. James shifts the focus from the *control* of the small object to its *destructive potential.*

While James 3:6 has several exegetical difficulties, the focus on the likelihood of the tongue's wickedness remains clear. For each difficulty, I will present the most compelling views.[12]

James negatively describes the tongue in five ways. The first,

---

9 This is the first time James uses the term for 'tongue'.

10 For other examples of boasting used in a negative sense, see Psalm 52:1; 73:9; 94:4.

11 The term could refer to a *pile of wood* rather than a forest. See Ropes, *St. James*, 232–3; McCartney, *James*, 185. Either way, the point remains: a small item can destroy a larger one.

12 For a discussion of the different exegetical issues, see Martin, *James*, 114–16; Allison, *James*, 534–42; Dibelius, *James*, 193–8.

'the tongue also is a fire', reminds us of 3:5b (see also Proverbs 16:27). This metaphor is effective: the tongue can cause pervasive destruction if left uncontrolled. It recalls a United States Forest Service campaign featuring Smokey Bear, who stresses that the responsibility to prevent forest fires lies only with us. Smokey urges campers to ensure their sites are free of fire hazards, such as warm embers or used cigarettes, reminding us of the power we have to make a difference. Like a small spark, spoken words can destroy lives. Many have experienced how a hurtful remark can linger in the memory for years and negatively impact one's whole life.

Second, James describes the tongue as 'a world of evil among the parts of the body'. James's use of 'world' elsewhere (1:27; 2:5; 4:4) refers to a realm of wickedness. This sense is corroborated in James 3:6 by the term 'evil'.[13] Thus, James is likely communicating that the tongue is the evil realm among the rest of our body parts, being often associated with wickedness.[14] Jesus had a similar teaching in Mark 7:14–23, stating, 'What comes out of a person is what defiles them.'

Third, in stating that the tongue 'corrupts the whole body', James uses a metaphor of a stain or blemish.[15] This recalls the statement that a pious person bridles the tongue and keeps 'oneself from being polluted by the world' (1:26–7). The tongue defiles one's true dedication to God; one's entire self can be corrupted.

Fourth, the tongue 'sets the whole course of one's life on fire'. The stakes have been raised even higher. Returning to the imagery of fire (3:5–6a), James reiterates that the tongue can have a tremendous destructive impact. The 'whole course of one's life' probably refers to a life cycle, or to the 'ups and downs' of a life

13 The term *adikia* is the negated form of the word family that indicates righteousness in James (see 1:20; 2:21–5).

14 Blomberg and Kamell, *James*, 157–8; Martin, *James*, 114–15.

15 See the verb form in 2 Peter 2:13; Ephesians 5:27. In Jude 23, it refers to a garment being soiled.

from beginning to end.[16] Thus, the tongue can corrupt not only the whole self, but also the entire length of one's life.

Fifth, the tongue 'is itself set on fire by hell'. The term 'hell' is *Gehenna*, referring to the valley of Hinnom surrounding Jerusalem. The valley was associated with death, wickedness and fire in the Old Testament.[17] Jesus associated Gehenna with the eternal torment of divine judgment.[18] Considering the sayings of Jesus, James's reference to the tongue in Gehenna likely refers to *judgment*. The tongue suffers the flames of hell because of its wickedness.[19] James's warning about strict judgment (3:1) is grave: left out of control, the tongue can destroy lives and can lead to the fires of Gehenna.

## *4. The difficulty of keeping the tongue in check • James 3:7–8*

After the harrowing descriptions of the tongue's destructive power, James discusses how difficult it is to control it. He has already discussed this difficulty in James 3:2, stating that a person who keeps their whole body in check is 'perfect'. In James 3:7–8 he contrasts the animal kingdom and the tongue.

---

16 Moo, *The Letter of James*, 197–8. Moo explains the difficulty in deciphering this phrase.

17 See 2 Kings 16:3; 23:8–10; 2 Chronicles 33:6.

18 See Matthew 5:22, (especially) 29–30; 10:28; 18:9; 23:15, 33; Mark 9:43, 45, 47; Luke 12:5. For an accessible explanation of the significance of Gehenna, see David A. Croteau, *Urban Legends of the New Testament: 40 Common Misconceptions* (Nashville: B&H Academic, 2015), 49–52.

19 This view is preferred to the interpretation that Satan, the occupant of hell, gives wicked power to the tongue. For the different views, see Moo, *The Letter of James*, 198; Martin, *James*, 116; Cheung and Spurgeon, *James*, 68; Richard Bauckham, *The Fate of the Dead: Studies on the Jewish and Christian Apocalypses* (Leiden: Brill, 1998), 119–31.

In James 3:7, our author describes 'all kinds of animals, birds, reptiles and sea creatures'. The language of humans having control over the entire animal kingdom accords with the creation account:[20]

> Then God said, 'Let us make mankind in our image, in our likeness, so that they may rule over the fish in the sea and the birds in the sky, over the livestock and all the wild animals, and over all the creatures that move along the ground.' (Genesis 1:26)

The repetition of 'tamed' in 3:7 emphasises that wild animals need subduing. The usage of both present and past tense shows that taming has continuously occurred since creation, according to the divine mandate. Not only can humans tame animals, but we have also been doing so for all time.

The all-encompassing declaration sets up a stark contrast with the tongue, found in James 3:8. Even though humans can tame all animals, no human can tame the tongue. This creates an irony: the animal world, outside our bodies, can be tamed. But the tongue, within our own bodies (see 3:6), escapes our mastery.

Note three observations here. First, James 3:8 does not contradict the earlier statement in 3:2 that a perfect person can bridle his whole body (also see 1:26). One must remember that 'perfect' to James does not necessarily connote sinlessness, but maturity.[21] Second, James may be using hyperbole, exaggerating with 'no human being', to describe the difficulty of controlling the tongue.[22] Third, the fact that James mentions 'no human being' implies that one must look outside the human world to tame

20 Moo, *The Letter of James*, 199.

21 See the commentary at 1:4 regarding the plural form, *teleioi*.

22 J. L. P. Wolmarans, 'The Tongue Guiding the Body: The Anthropological Presuppositions of James 3:1–12', *Neotestamentica* 26, no. 2 (1992): 526.

the tongue: it is God who can control the tongue for us.[23] Ultimately, James's point stands: the tongue is extremely difficult to keep in check.

James ends this subsection with two more descriptors of the tongue in 3:8b: 'a restless evil, full of deadly poison'. The word for 'restless' is the same term used in 1:8 to refer to the double-minded person who cannot decide where to settle his loyalty. In the same way, the tongue is unstable and difficult to control. Its wickedness is enhanced by this adjective, which James condemns in both contexts. The reference to deadly poison is apt since it is such a destructive force and can lead to fiery condemnation. This imagery holds a particular irony; it is the tongue that can taste life-giving food and drink, yet it can cause death.[24] Indeed, there are deadly results if the tongue is left without rein.

## 5. *Using the tongue singly to bless, not curse • James 3:9–12*

After discussing the difficulty of controlling the tongue, James urges his hearers to use the tongue for one purpose alone: not to curse, but to bless. A thread running through James 3:9–12 is the tongue's two opposite functions: to bless and to curse. This is consistent with James's motif of choosing the better of two ways. It also echoes the condemnation of someone who is 'double-minded' (1:8, also 4:8).

First, James states in 3:9 that the tongue is used to praise God and to curse others. These are the two extremes of speech – the

23 As suggested by Blomberg and Kamell, *James*, 160. This interpretation relies on 'humans' being paired with 'no one' ('no one of humans') rather than with the tongue ('the tongue of humans'). James has already been discussing the human tongue, so the former is more likely; 'tongue' would not need a qualifier.

24 Blomberg and Kamell, 160.

most honourable and most dishonourable functions. The first phrase, 'praise our Lord and Father', echoes the Old Testament call to praise the Lord (Psalm 16:7; Deuteronomy 8:10; Judges 5:2). The second is that we curse other humans. Like in 3:1, James includes himself with the plural 'we'. The repetition of 'human' from 3:8 reminds the hearers of the contrast between the Creator and creation, but also of the status of being image-bearers, which James makes explicit. There is an irony here: we bless God, but we do not bless those made in God's image. Again, James appeals to the creation account. Whether or not they are Christ-followers, all humans are created to reflect God. The 'curse' is not just for formal pronouncements, but for denouncing and evil speech. Later in the epistle, James will condemn ways to use words against others, like quarrels (4:1–2), slandering (4:11) and grumbling against one another (5:9).

To emphasise his point, in 3:10 James writes that the two functions come out of the same mouth. The tongue is duplicitous, which James states 'should not be' (3:10). James's condemnation of the tongue's double use echoes the double-minded person asking God for wisdom in 1:6–8. The message is similar: choose the way that is pleasing to the Lord. The tongue 'should' have a single use, only for blessing.

James illustrates his point in 3:11–12 by giving several examples from creation. Each example shows that God designed a unit for a singular function. The first example speaks against double use: 'Can both fresh water and salt water flow from the same spring?'[25] James expects a 'no' answer: the tongue should not have two functions, but one.

The illustrations in James 3:12 convey a related point: a created

25 There is a striking parallel with Jesus's teaching in Matthew 7:18–19 and Luke 6:43–4. However, James's point differs from Jesus's. While Jesus explains that bad trees are thrown into the fire, James writes that a tree for a particular fruit does not produce a different kind as well – its created function is singular.

item cannot produce something other than its created function: a fig tree cannot bear olives, nor can a grapevine bear figs. A salt spring cannot produce fresh water. These acts would go against their created functions. Likewise, it goes against the Creator's design for the human tongue to curse other humans. James urges his hearers to reflect the Creator's intent: only use the tongue to bless. This is consistent with Jesus's command to 'bless those who curse you' (Luke 6:28; see also Matthew 5:44), which is echoed in Paul's teaching (Romans 12:14).

The cumulative message of this subsection, in accordance with James's 'be like this and not that' motif, is that the tongue is to be used for blessing only. It 'should not be' that the tongue is used doubly for blessing and cursing. Like the double-minded (1:8; 4:8), this double use of the tongue is condemned.

A section that started with the exhortation that few should become teachers (3:1) widened to a discussion about the tongue in general. The tongue has great power disproportionate to its size (3:3–6); it is difficult to keep in check (3:7–8) and it should be used singly to bless (3:9–12).

In today's media-saturated world, communication is more accessible than ever. With the general teaching about the tongue, those who teach and preach ought to watch their speech, wary of its destructive potential. The tongue should be wielded with reverence and utmost care.

# 8

# Display Wisdom from Above

## JAMES 3:13–18

James 3:13–18, which discusses two kinds of wisdom, is distinct from James 3:1–12.[1] It has grammatical ties within the passage that hold it together, as well as the themes of wisdom, peace and fruit. These themes do not occur in 3:1–12. Also, 3:13–18 does not continue the dominant theme of 3:1–12, the tongue.[2] Some might consider the content of 3:13–18 to apply to teachers, using 3:1 as an introduction to this content.[3] However, the content about the tongue in 3:3–12 is stated in more general terms. Also, heavenly wisdom, the main topic of 3:13–18, is accessible to all Christ-followers (see 1:5).

Despite its distinctiveness from James 3:1–12, James 3:13–18 links to material in James 1–2. This suggests that the content in 3:13–18 is likely serving as a summarising transition, reminding the hearers of the main ideas in the first half of the epistle.[4] He

1 To be sure, James links 3:13–18 back to 3:1–12, sharing 'bitter' in 3:14 (the term for salt water in 3:11), and the cognate terms 'restless'/'disorder' (3:8; 3:16). But their different usages suggest that they are catchwords, which link disparate sections of text, rather than evidence of a continuing section of thought. See the discussion of catchwords in James in the section 'The cohesiveness of James 1' in chapter 1 of this book.

2 See my case for the distinctiveness of James 3:13–18 in *Eschatological Approval*, 77–81.

3 See, for example, McKnight, *Letter of James*, 55; Ashby L. Camp, 'Another View on the Structure of James', *Restoration Quarterly* 36 (1994): 116–18.

4 There is a more detailed list in Eng, *Eschatological Approval*, 80–81.

revisits (a) an appeal to wisdom, first found in 1:5; (b) a call to show what is unseen through outward deeds, echoing 2:18; (c) the charge to act in humility (3:13), a phrase first introduced in 1:21; (d) a warning against deception in 3:14, introduced in 1:22 and 1:26; (e) a valuable gift from above in 3:15 and 3:17, echoing the same phrase in 1:17; and (f) the call for *mercy* in 3:17, found in the calls to care for the less fortunate in 1:27 and 2:13. With so many reminders of James 1–2, James groups them as behaviours that characterise wisdom from above.

James 3:13–18 also contains material that connects it with the content in James 4:1–10. It introduces the condemnation of 'envy' (3:14, 16), which will be revisited in 4:2 (NIV: 'covet') and 4:5 ('jealously').[5] Furthermore, there is a connection between 'envy' and 'friendship' (see 4:4) commonly found in Greek and Jewish writings.[6]

With its connections to previous material occurring in the epistle's first half as well as its previewing of material in James 4, James 3:13–18 most likely serves as a 'bridge'. It summarises the actions that come from heavenly wisdom and contrasts this with earthly wisdom, preparing the hearers for the rebuke that is to come in James 4.[7]

Indeed, to live in adherence to the Lord's ways, one needs heavenly wisdom. In James 3:13–18, James presents the contrast between this true wisdom and its 'counterfeit'.[8] Here, James will describe both earthly and heavenly wisdom, along with the practical outworking of following each of them.

---

5 Luke Timothy Johnson, 'James 3:13–4:10 and the Topos Περὶ Φθόνου', *Novum Testamentum* 25 (1983): 345.

6 Johnson, 333–46. Also Hartin, *James*, 203–7.

7 Taylor, *Text-Linguistic*, 116. In accordance with these observations, Varner calls James 3:13–18 the 'thematic peak' of the epistle, expressing the main themes of the letter. Varner, *James*, 243–6.

8 Peter H. Davids, *A Theology of James, Peter, and Jude: Living in the Light of the Coming King* (Grand Rapids: Zondervan, 2014), 62.

This summarising transition section unfolds in three steps. First, James challenges the hearers who claim to be wise to show their wisdom from their good deeds (3:13). Second, he warns his hearers against following earthly wisdom (3:14–16). Third, he describes wisdom from heaven and its results (3:17–18).

*Two kinds of wisdom*

**13** Who is wise and understanding
among you? Let them show it by their
good life, by deeds done in the humility that comes from wisdom. **14** But if
you harbour bitter envy and selfish
ambition in your hearts, do not boast
about it or deny the truth. **15** Such
'wisdom' does not come down from
heaven but is earthly, unspiritual,
demonic. **16** For where you have envy
and selfish ambition, there you find
disorder and every evil practice.

**17** But the wisdom that comes
from heaven is first of all pure; then
peace-loving, considerate, submissive, full of mercy and good fruit,
impartial and sincere. **18** Peacemakers who sow in peace reap a
harvest of righteousness.

## 1. *Show your wisdom by your good deeds • James 3:13*

First, James calls his hearers to demonstrate their wisdom through their good deeds. In accordance with the epistle's thesis (1:12), the challenge here points to an evaluation. This call to show wisdom accords with key teachings found earlier in the epistle: being a doer of the word (1:22–5) and showing one's faith through good deeds (2:14–26). We must also recall that James 3:13–18 fits within the *inclusio* (2:12–13; 4:11–12) that urges the hearers to 'act' and be a 'doer' in light of coming judgment.

The descriptors 'wise and understanding' call to mind the figure of Solomon, who asked the Lord for wisdom and knowledge (2 Chronicles 1:10). Just like saving faith is paired with action (2:14–19), wisdom is not merely intellectual. In fact, as poet William Cowper wrote:

> Knowledge and Wisdom, far from being one,
> Have ofttimes no connection.[9]

Wisdom goes beyond knowledge and results in proper conduct, a 'good life' and 'deeds done in . . . humility'. Similarly, Solomon requested wisdom so that he may lead the people.[10]

James 3:13 is a 'show me' challenge, just like in 2:18. If one claims to be wise and understanding, it should come out in good conduct. This stands in contrast to showing favouritism to the rich (2:1–7) and leaving the tongue unbridled (3:2–6). One cannot claim to be wise without showing good deeds and humility.

For Christ-followers, whom should we seek for wisdom? Which person do we consult when our marriages are suffering, or our children are struggling? What do we look for in a person who can advise us on how to choose a career? James gives us guidance: someone with true wisdom shows it through humility and good deeds. Like James has affirmed in his letter, a wise and understanding person is generous, impartial, slow to anger and patient.

## *2. Warning against demonic wisdom • James 3:14–16*

In James 3:14–16, after issuing the challenge to show wisdom, James gives a warning against having earthly wisdom. This subsection has a chiastic structure – an 'ABA' format:

---

9 William Cowper, 'The Task', in *The Task, Table Talk, and Other Poems*, ed. James Robert Boyd (Cincinnati: A. S. Barnes & Company, 1857), 297.

10 'In humility' (*en prautēti*) also appears in James 1:21, referring to one's posture towards the word.

A: Envy or selfish ambition can lead to condemned speech.
  B: This kind of wisdom is 'earthly, unspiritual, demonic'.
A: Envy and selfish ambition lead to disorder and evil practices.

First, James urges his hearers not to act on their envy or selfish ambition. The condemned vices are compatible with one another. This 'envy' is not the jealousy of God (Exodus 34:14), but is 'bitter', indicating negative feelings over another's success.[11] Combined, the two vices evoke an image of people competing with one another, each fighting for their own rights, undermining one another in the process. This is the antithesis of humility that comes from wisdom.[12]

Like earlier in the epistle (1:19, 26; 3:2), James is especially concerned about speech ethics, teaching his hearers to refrain from boasting and denying the truth. These condemned actions come out of the inner self's envy and selfish ambition. A person who claims to be wise (3:13) but has these vices (3:14) is, in effect, 'living a lie'.[13] Their actions do not substantiate their claim. The notion that one's actions are a manifestation of the inner life is found in the sayings of Jesus, who also taught that one would be judged for these actions:

> For the mouth speaks what the heart is full of. A good man brings good things out of the good stored up in him, and an evil man brings evil things out of the evil stored up in him. But I tell you that everyone will have to give account on the day of judgment for every empty word they have spoken. (Matthew 12:34b–36)

11 Walter Bauer, 'Ζῆλος', in BDAG.

12 Blomberg and Kamell, *James*, 172.

13 Moo, *The Letter of James*, 171.

In the second saying (3:15), James states that someone whose speech is associated with envy and selfish ambition has the wrong sort of wisdom. He contrasts two kinds of wisdom: wisdom from above and earthly wisdom. He will describe the wisdom from above in 3:17–18, but first, he focuses on its antithesis.

Earthly wisdom is described with three adjectives, each progressively more negative,[14] and each deriving its meaning from its implied opposite.[15] The first one, 'earthly', connotes that its source is earth rather than heaven, with a decidedly negative nature. Paul also uses this adjective to describe enemies of Christ: 'their mind is set on earthly things' (Philippians 3:19). Second, such wisdom is 'unspiritual'. Here, the term describes the natural world in contrast to the ways of God.[16] Jude uses the same adjective (NIV: 'natural') to describe divisive people who 'do not have the Spirit' (Jude 19). A term that captures the negative connotation is 'worldly'.[17] The third descriptor is the most pejorative: 'demonic'. The association with demons makes James's condemnation the most explicit. James has already mentioned demons (2:19) and Gehenna (3:6). Envy and selfish ambition do not reflect wisdom from God, but have their source in the realm of wickedness. Each of the three adjectives acknowledges the source – such wisdom is not from God. In fact, this is not true wisdom at all. As James established early in the epistle, wisdom comes from God (1:5).

In James 3:16, the third saying about demonic wisdom, our author again discusses the manifestation of envy and selfish ambition. This time the description is not focused on speech ethics, but on the more general results of these vices. Also, unlike 3:14,

14 Spencer, *A Commentary on James*, 190.

15 Douglas J. Moo, *Letter of James: Introduction and Commentary* (Grand Rapids: InterVarsity Press, 1985), 138.

16 'Ψυχικός', in BDAG.

17 Paul also uses it negatively in 1 Corinthians 2:14.

there is no command; it is a declaration of the negative effects of such wisdom.

The first result of envy and selfish ambition is 'disorder'. As discussed above, this term was introduced earlier in the adjective form, describing the double-minded person as 'unstable' (1:8). It is also used in the negative description of the tongue in 3:8 (NIV: 'restless'). This term is featured in the LXX at the creation account to describe the earth (Genesis 1:2) – it is God who brings order to the chaos. Indeed, disorder is antithetical to God's ways: 'For God is not a God of disorder but of peace' (1 Corinthians 14:33).

Disorder does not just occur in an individual, but also in relationships with others. This sort of disorder will be revisited in the 'fights and quarrels' in 4:1. As they were associated with competition and destructive egoism in 3:15, we see that the results of envy and selfish ambition negatively impact the community – there is no peace. The manifestation of godly wisdom brings order and peace to the community (or communities) of James's hearers.[18]

The second result of envy and selfish ambition is 'every evil practice'. These actions displease God, and those who practise them will be condemned. Consistent with the letter's thesis (1:12), there is an evaluation: judgment. Here, James sums up the previous material of the epistle, the acts that he prohibits: accusing God of temptation (1:13–15), becoming angry (1:19), failing to do the word (1:22–3), showing partiality to the rich (2:1–9), not caring for someone in need (2:15–16) and using the tongue to curse others (3:9–12).[19] These are the evil practices included in the results of envy and selfishness.

18 Moo suggests that the focus of this wisdom is order and peace within the *church*. See *The Letter of James*, 224.

19 Spencer, *A Commentary on James*, 192.

## *3. Description and results of heavenly wisdom • James 3:17–18*

After describing a 'wisdom' that is condemned, James goes on to describe the wisdom from above (3:17). As we will see, he gives a series of descriptors of heavenly wisdom, grouping them in a particular way.

Before the series of adjectives for heavenly wisdom, James singles out one of them from the others: 'first of all pure'. Purity connotes 'free from moral pollution',[20] as it is used for God's words (Psalm 12:6),[21] and the ways of the righteous (Proverbs 15:26; 21:8) in the LXX, as well as moral purity in the New Testament (for example, 2 Corinthians 7:11; Philippians 4:8; Titus 2:5; 1 John 3:3). It also has a connotation with ritual purity (for example, Leviticus 13:47–58; Numbers 19:11–13; Deuteronomy 23:10–14), which recalls being free from the world's pollution in James 1:27. All of this points to what is unseen: one has purity in the inner life.

Following the motif that the unseen leads to the seen, the rest of the descriptors in James 3:17–18 are outward expressions of this inner purity.[22] The next adjective is 'peace-loving'. This is a logical conclusion, as envy and selfish ambition do not lead to peace. Peace was a significant value in Israel, making '*Shalom*' a common saying of blessing in Hebrew. This value of peace is reflected in the New Testament (such as in Luke 24:36; Romans 1:7; James 2:16; 1 Peter 5:14). Jesus identified the peacemakers as

---

20 Darian Lockett, *Purity and Worldview in the Epistle of James* (London: T&T Clark, 2008), 128.

21 Psalm 11:7 in the LXX.

22 See James 2:18 and 3:14–16. For more on this view that the rest of the list flows from the first descriptor, see Ropes, *St. James*, 249; Joseph B. Mayor, *The Epistle of St. James: The Greek Text with Introduction Notes and Comments*, (Third edition; London: MacMillan, 1910), 130.

blessed in his kingdom (Matthew 5:9). 'Peace-loving' contrasts being contentious or strife-filled, which James will condemn in 4:1.

Next, wisdom from above is 'considerate'. This adjective is a 'near synonym' of 'humility' in 3:13,[23] and refers to yielding, not insisting on every right. The next descriptor is 'submissive', referring to obedience and compliance. These adjectives for heavenly wisdom are set in contrast to the demonic wisdom, with its envy and selfishness (3:15). Again, James regards highly the virtues that impact others in the community.

In Greek, the adjectives rendered 'pure, peace-loving, considerate' and 'submissive' have alliteration and assonance, starting with and containing similar sounds.[24] The author's choice of these words shows intentionality, since each of them could have synonyms. The similar sounds probably aid the memory of the hearers, as the epistle was likely to be read aloud. The parallel sounds also tie together these adjectives that have purity as a prerequisite. This is fitting, since they demonstrate someone being free from the world's defiling characteristics (see 1:27).

The next adjective, 'full', serves to group two abstract concepts. The first is 'mercy', a noun with similar sounds as the group of four adjectives.[25] James has already given a strong statement regarding the value of mercy in 2:12–13, which we have discussed as a preview for the content following it. The logic follows: the person who shows mercy to the poor will triumph over condemnation (2:13), as it demonstrates wisdom from above (3:17).

The second noun that goes with 'full' is 'good fruit'. While James had referred to his hearers themselves as 'firstfruits' (1:18),

---

23 Allison, *James*, 582.

24 *epeita*, *eirēnikē*, *epieikēs*, *eupeithēs*. The term for mercy is *eleos*.

25 The alliteration and assonance in 3:17 suggests an even stronger contrast with 3:14–16. See Herbert W. Bateman IV and William Varner, *James: An Exegetical Guide for Preaching and Teaching* (Kregel Academic, 2022), 202.

the qualifier 'good' points to their actions. The concept of fruit as deeds fits well with the discussion of faith and deeds in 2:14–25 and the actions of the tongue in 3:1–12. The phrase 'good fruit' recalls Jesus's teaching (such as Matthew 3:8, 10; Luke 3:8–9), especially his declaration that 'a good tree cannot bear bad fruit, and a bad tree cannot bear good fruit' (Matthew 7:18). In the same spirit as the 'show me' challenges in James, 'fruit' are the visible manifestations of what is on the inside – in this case, wisdom from above. These deeds are done in accordance with being 'peace-loving', considerate' and 'submissive'.

The last two adjectives in James 3:17, 'impartial' and 'sincere', are also grouped with their similar initial and final sounds.[26] Both terms are negating in nature: they each describe the absence of a vice. The first, the descriptor 'impartial' suggests *non-judging*.[27] James will condemn judging again later in 4:11–12. As discussed above, the epistle has a repeated theme of judgment; when it is used of people as the subject, it is condemned.

The second adjective, 'sincere', is more accurately rendered 'without insincerity'.[28] Note the root of the word *hypocrite* in *anypokritos* – wisdom from above is unhypocritical. Again, James affirms that the unseen positive attributes result in good deeds, positively impacting the community.

Much like his practice in previous sections, James ends with a timeless truth. In contrast to the envy and disorder of demonic wisdom (and the fights and quarrels in 4:1–2), heavenly wisdom brings peace to the community. By making peace, followers of Christ produce fruit, or a 'harvest'.[29] James's concept here is

26 *Adiakritos* and *anypokritos*.

27 The term *adiakritos* is the absence of the vice in 1:6 and 2:4 (*diakrinō*) that makes a person *double-minded* (1:8) or *a judge with evil thoughts* (2:4). In Greek words with the alpha-privative, the initial letter expresses negation, as shown in words like *amoral* and *atheist*.

28 J. Alec Motyer, *The Message of James* (Leicester: InterVarsity Press, 1985), 136.

29 The Greek text is ambiguous about the identity of the sower(s): it could

consistent with the sayings of Jesus (Matthew 3:8–10; 12:33–7; Luke 3:8–9). In the Sermon on the Mount/Plain, to which James repeatedly alludes, 'fruit' has eschatological consequences: a tree with bad fruit is thrown into the fire (Matthew 7:16–20; Luke 6:43–4).[30] Thus, in consistency with the thesis (1:12), James gives the message that heavenly wisdom leads to good deeds, which leads to favourable end-time judgment and reward.

---

be the peacemakers themselves, or it could be God (as the NRSV indicates). The repetition of 'fruit' from 3:17 ('harvest' in the NIV) and its usage in the sayings of Jesus suggest that the people who sow are the ones who produce fruit. See a possible parallel in Hosea 10:12, and my analysis in *Eschatological Approval*, 161–3.

30 Bauckham suggests eschatological reward in James 3:18, in connection with 1:12. See *James: Wisdom of James, Disciple of Jesus the Sage* (London: Routledge, 1999), 108.

# 9

# Submit to God

## JAMES 4:1–12

James 4:1–12 concludes the main part of the body of the epistle, and urges the hearers to adhere to God's ways with eschatological judgment in view. As we have discussed earlier, James 4:11–12 marks the end of the *inclusio* that began with 2:12–13, with its clustering of terms for 'judge' and 'law' and the prominence of speech ethics.

In several ways, James 4:1–12 builds on the previous section. James 4:1 contains the phrase 'among you', which also appeared in 3:13. In James 3:13–18, the author presented a contrast between two types of wisdom, affirming the wisdom from above and condemning the demonic 'wisdom' from the earth. This content at the beginning of James 4 becomes more direct as James uses strong language and a harsh tone to exhort his followers.[1]

This subsection can be seen as the conclusion of the main body (4:1–10) and as the transitionary statements that close the *inclusio* (4:11–12). Elements of 4:1–10 give the unit cohesion: from the theme of quarrels and fighting to the contrast between adhering to and opposing God. In accordance with the epistle's thesis (1:12), the hearers again receive the message that they are to choose the better of two alternatives, which will lead to

1 Varner designates James 4:1–10 as the *hortatory peak* of the epistle, coming after the *thematic peak* of 3:13–18. See William C. Varner, *The Book of James: A New Perspective* (Woodlands, TX: Kress Biblical Resources, 2010), 28–35.

blessing in the end. They are then exhorted to submit to God, who is the one true judge (4:11–12).

*Submit yourselves to God*

**4** What causes fights and quarrels
among you? Don't they come
from your desires that battle within
you? **2** You desire but do not have, so
you kill. You covet but you cannot get
what you want, so you quarrel and
fight. You do not have because you
do not ask God. **3** When you ask, you
do not receive, because you ask with
wrong motives, that you may spend
what you get on your pleasures.

**4** You adulterous people,[a] don't
you know that friendship with the
world means enmity against God?
Therefore, anyone who chooses to
be a friend of the world becomes
an enemy of God. **5** Or do you think
Scripture says without reason that he
jealously longs for the spirit he has
caused to dwell in us[b]? **6** But he gives
us more grace. That is why Scripture
says:

'God opposes the proud
but shows favour to the
humble.'[c]

**7** Submit yourselves, then, to God.
Resist the devil, and he will flee from
you. **8** Come near to God and he will
come near to you. Wash your hands,
you sinners, and purify your hearts,
you double-minded. **9** Grieve, mourn
and wail. Change your laughter to
mourning and your joy to gloom.
**10** Humble yourselves before the
Lord, and he will lift you up.

**11** Brothers and sisters, do not
slander one another. Anyone who
speaks against a brother or sister[d]
or judges them speaks against the
law and judges it. When you judge
the law, you are not keeping it, but
sitting in judgment on it. **12** There is
only one Lawgiver and Judge, the
one who is able to save and destroy.
But you – who are you to judge your
neighbour?

---

**a** 4 An allusion to covenant unfaithfulness; see Hosea 3:1.
**b** 5 Or *that the spirit he caused to dwell in us envies intensely;* or *that the Spirit he caused to dwell in us longs jealously*
**c** 6 Prov. 3:34
**d** 11 The Greek word for *brother or sister* (*adelphos*) refers here to a believer, whether man or woman, as part of God's family.

## 1. *Pursuing selfish desires causes strife • James 4:1–3*

Before describing the benefits of submitting to God, James first presents the antithesis. He points out how his hearers' behaviour in the community is not only incompatible with allegiance to God, but also even detrimental to it.

First, James begins the subsection with a question, much like he does in 2:14. In his question, he points out the 'fights and quarrels' among his hearers. Just like the two kinds of wisdom in 3:13–18, their strife must have a source. He follows with another question, this time a rhetorical one that forms a forceful indictment.[2] He implies a 'yes' answer: 'Don't they come from your desires that battle within you?'

Note that James's comments address the community – the fights and quarrels occur in relationships with others. Again, James's exhortations are to be lived out in the context of their communities, like much of the epistle's previous content (1:27; 2:1–7, 16; 3:10, 13–18). 'Fights and quarrels' stand in contrast to the terms 'peace-loving', 'peacemakers' and 'peace' in 3:17–18.

It is unclear whether the 'fights and quarrels' refer to only verbal quarrels or physical violence. On the one hand, the context in James favours the former, as it highlights the destructive power of the tongue (3:3–12; 4:11–12).[3] Indeed, James has repeatedly discussed the crucial nature of speech ethics. Also, every other New Testament instance of 'quarrels' is figurative, referring to verbal disputes.[4] On the other hand, nothing precludes the possibility of physical violence. James and the early church

2 James uses a diatribe style, alliteration and homoioteleuton (similar word endings) here in 4:1 for rhetorical effect. See Varner, *James*, 272–3.

3 For this view, see Moo, *The Letter of James*, 225.

4 See 2 Corinthians 7:5; 2 Timothy 2:23; Titus 3:9. The use is figurative, since the term can refer to physical battles, and the verb form is largely used for physical combat outside the New Testament. See 'Μάχομαι', in BDAG.

were indeed engaged in a 'Zealot-infested society' and violence occurred in religious contexts.[5] Also, every other New Testament instance of 'fights' refers to military battles.[6] A third option can solve this conundrum: James is addressing verbal disputes, with the possibility that the desires and coveting (4:2) could lead to physical violence. Furthermore, the present tense verbs in 4:1–3 suggest that James is not addressing a particular situation.[7] An examination of verse 2 below will help bolster the view that James is considering the possibility of physical violence.

With the second question of James 4:1, the author continues the theme that one's outward behaviour is a manifestation of what is inside. The 'fights and quarrels' are a result of the hearers following their evil desires, much like good deeds result from faith (2:18) and a good life results from wisdom from above (3:13). Here, evil desires produce condemned behaviour. In the prologue, James introduced the concept that sin is birthed from one's 'desire' (1:14–15). Here, the distinct term for 'desire' refers specifically to the experience of sensual pleasure.[8]

James writes that these pleasures have a battle, and the language here refers to waging war. While James addresses his plural audience ('within you'), the location of these battles is not specified. The waging of war could be occurring within an individual, like a battle between selfishness and righteousness,[9] or occurring between members of the church body.[10] The context favours the former for three reasons. First, the phrase translated 'within you'

5 See Martin, *James*, 144. Martin holds the view that James is warning against physical violence and even literal murder (see James 4:2). McKnight cites Paul's example of religious violence. See *Letter of James*, 322.

6 The Greek term is *polemoi*, from which we get the English term 'polemic'. See, for example, Matthew 24:6; 1 Corinthians 14:8; Revelation 20:8.

7 Chris A. Vlachos, *James* (Nashville: B&H Academic, 2013), 129.

8 'Ἡδονή', in BDAG. Note the root of 'hedonism' in *hēdonē*.

9 For this view, see Davids, *Epistle of James*, 324; Moo, *The Letter of James*, 227.

10 See Martin, *James*, 144–5; Spencer, *A Commentary on James*, 211.

is woodenly 'in your members', and James used the term for 'member' to refer to the tongue's relation to the human body in 3:5–6. Second, there is a parallel statement in 1 Peter 2:11, which uses the same verb for 'sinful desires, which wage war against your soul'.[11] Third, James has already discussed conflicts within the community in the first question in 4:1. Here, in the second question, he is discussing their source.

James's condemnation of following one's desires is consistent with a biblical theme. 'The heart is deceitful above all things' (Jeremiah 17:9), and one should trust God rather than one's own understanding (Proverbs 3:5). Jesus taught that the heart – the inner self – is the source of evil thoughts like murder, theft and adultery (Matthew 15:19).

While the hyper-individualism that characterises much of the Global West is often expressed in sayings like 'you do you' and 'follow your heart', the Bible urges its hearers to follow the Lord. While modern values might promote the mantra 'be yourself', Jesus teaches that, in order to follow him, the self must be denied (Matthew 16:24). Indeed, the apostle Paul teaches that the flesh and the Spirit are at odds with each other (Galatians 5:17).

James 4:2a is difficult to delineate, because of its lack of conjunctions. The NIV renders this as two parallel statements, interpretatively adding the conjunctions 'so':

> You desire but do not have, so you kill.
> You covet but you cannot get what you want,
> so you quarrel and fight.

William F. Brosend points out the parallel concepts that James 4:2a has with the two rhetorical questions in 4:1, proposing this chiastic structure:[12]

11 Vlachos, *James*, 130.

12 I have substituted the NIV text here. See William F. Brosend II, *James &*

A What causes fights and quarrels among you?
B Don't they come from your desires that battle within you?
C You desire but do not have, so
C' you kill. You covet
B' but you cannot get what you want, so
A' you quarrel and fight.

Brosend's proposal is intriguing, as it places the focus on the drastic behaviour of murder. However, the double parallel statements better account for the unfulfilled desires. Ultimately, with either delineation of the sayings, the behaviours involving fights, quarrels, killing and coveting are clearly condemned. Also, while 'desire' can be used for any general type of longing, the immediate context in 4:2 indicates that James is using it in a negative sense.[13]

To be sure, the term 'kill' (*phoneuō*) carries a negative connotation.[14] Rather than describing the ending of life for any reason,[15] it describes *murder*, as it is used in the New Testament in quotations of the Torah law 'You shall not murder.' Jesus's teaching on this commandment is especially notable since James often echoes the sayings of Jesus (see Matthew 5:21; Mark 10:19; Luke 18:20). Notably, James uses this same word in both quoting

*Jude* (Cambridge: Cambridge University Press, 2004), 107–8.

13 James also uses the noun form (*epithymia*) in 1:14–15. Note that it differs from the term *hēdonē*, also translated 'desire', in 4:1.

14 Erasmus proposed that the verb – inflected as *phoneuete* here – is not original, but that the original is *phthoneite* – 'you envy'. This possibility is attractive, since it would naturally pair with *zēloute* ('you are jealous', rendered as 'covet' in the NIV). However, this is conjecture, as there is no evidence in our manuscript tradition for *phthoneite*. For details, see Allison, *James*, 602 n70; 'Φονεύω', in BDAG.

15 A much more common New Testament word for 'kill is *apokteinō*, which does not necessarily indicate murder. See its usage in Matthew 10:28; Luke 13:4; Revelation 6:8.

the commandment in 2:11–12 and describing the condemned behaviour of the rich in 5:6.

James gives the motivation for murder: unfulfilled desires. It is selfish longings that lead people to drastic action. Here, James specifies the selfish desire as coveting: desiring to take what someone else has. He earlier quoted Leviticus 19:18, the command to 'love your neighbour as yourself' (James 2:8). Part of loving a neighbour means not to covet, nor to desire what a neighbour has.[16]

While James's description of murder could be merely metaphorical, nothing in the text indicates something other than actual murder. It is indeed possible that covetous desires lead to murder. In the account of Naboth the Jezreelite (1 Kings 21:1–16), Ahab and Jezebel coveted Naboth's vineyard. When they, like James describes, could not get what they wanted, they had Naboth stoned to death.[17] James's words likely also recall King David having Uriah killed because he coveted Bathsheba (2 Samuel 11). Such murders still happen today. In 2018, a high-profile case involved a man in India who constructed a bomb that killed two people. His motivation was jealousy over his colleague receiving his position.[18]

As discussed above, the church was birthed in societies where physical violence was frequent. After all, illicit desire develops into sin, which leads to death (James 1:14–15). Similarly, James

16 Philo and others considered Leviticus 19:18 to be the summary of the second half of the Ten Commandments, including the prohibition of coveting. See Allison, *James*, 601.

17 Notably, the LXX indicates that, according to Elijah, Ahab has *murdered (phoneuō)* Naboth (1 Kings 20:19, LXX).

18 DC Correspondent, 'Odisha Parcel Bomb Case: Lecturer Plotted Attack Out of "Jealousy", Say Cops', *Deccan Chronicle*, 26 April 2018, www.deccanchronicle.com/nation/current-affairs/260418/odisha-parcel-bomb-case-lecturer-plotted-attack-out-of-jealousy-sa.html (accessed 24 July 2024). As highlighted in Cheung and Spurgeon, *James*, 82.

states in 4:2 that unchecked selfish desires could lead to death – murder. As also discussed above, the present tense suggests that there is no particular situation of actual murder that James has in mind.[19] However, like the 'fights' in James 4:1 can include physical combat, the selfish desires can, when left unhindered, lead to murder.

The 'fights and quarrels', which bookend the sayings that also describe the desires and murder, are the result of unmet wants. Whether the hearers desire material goods, esteem, knowledge or power is unclear. But James specifies that these desires are selfish. If they are not curbed, they can lead to destructive acts. We may not have experienced murder, but all of us have experienced conflict within a community – and it is destructive.

Ultimately, murder occurs because of desire that is misdirected. These underprivileged hearers of James should not covet a neighbour's things, but rather present their requests to God. James writes, 'You do not have because you do not ask God.'[20] Earlier, James described God as generous and not finding fault in the person requesting wisdom (1:5). This teaching from James recalls Jesus's teaching in the Sermon on the Mount: 'Ask and it will be given to you . . . for everyone who asks receives' (Matthew 7:7–8).

But the modern reader of James would have an objection to this teaching: those who pray still often have their desires unfulfilled. What is happening when God does not grant our requests? In 4:3, James explains, 'You do not receive, because you ask with wrong motives, that you may spend what you get on your pleasures.' James reaffirms that their desires are only for their pleasure. They do not receive what they want because of their selfish intentions.

---

19 Moo rightly points out that 'it strains credulity to suppose that James would pass so quickly over so serious a matter within the community' as murder. See Moo, *The Letter of James*, 230.

20 The Greek omits *God*, but this is implied by the next statement.

Here, James speaks against the Prosperity Gospel, a false teaching that thrives in many cultures. The Prosperity Gospel appeals to the human longing for health and wealth. But, as Costi Hinn warns, 'If we choose to serve our appetites and indulge in nothing but our pleasures, we will reap the outcome of those selfish choices.'[21] Indeed, God opposes this selfishness, and will not grant selfish requests.

Indeed, God does not grant every request. The teaching about 'asking and knocking' in the Sermon on the Mount is set within the context of 'good gifts' (Matthew 7:11), using an illustration from parenting. Even we, who are evil, give good gifts to our children. Likewise, the Father will 'give good gifts to those who ask him'. The logic implies that if God, who is not evil, does not grant the request, the request must not be 'good'. Indeed, James wrote earlier (1:17) that 'every good and perfect gift' is from the Father.

Receiving one's selfish desires can have disastrous consequences. In his book *Don't Follow Your Heart*, Thaddeus J. Williams refers to following one's emotions as 'self-worship', and urges readers to display the fruit of the Spirit instead. He writes that seeking one's own desires – the content of many commencement addresses and Oscar acceptance speeches – is 'terrible advice . . . We don't hear such fuzzy sentiments from people who have followed their hearts straight to the divorce court, the detox clinic, or the prison yard.'[22]

This condemnation of the selfish desires in James 4:3 is even more poignant in light of the collectivistic cultures characterising the New Testament. Much like the Global East and South today, collectivistic societies place the needs of the group – the

21 Costi W. Hinn, *God, Greed, and the (Prosperity) Gospel: How Truth Overwhelms a Life Built on Lies* (Grand Rapids: Zondervan, 2019), 94.

22 Thaddeus J. Williams, *Don't Follow Your Heart: Boldly Breaking the Ten Commandments of Self-Worship* (Zondervan, 2023), 41.

family, clan and nation – above the needs of the individual. It would be disgraceful for an individual to put his or her own desires above the needs of others. This is the principle taught by James, and he teaches that their selfishness is the reason for their requests being denied.

In addition, in such other-centric (rather than self-centric) societies, group harmony is paramount. One is discouraged from 'making waves' or 'rocking the boat', so that peace is preserved. Since unmet selfish desires lead to fights and quarrels, as James states, then peace is destroyed by the selfishness of individuals. They have unthinkably placed their own desires above the needs of the group. The value espoused by such collectivistic societies is embodied by the *Star Trek* character Spock in the film *The Wrath of Khan*. To paraphrase Spock, the needs of the few are outweighed by the needs of the many.

The modern teacher or preacher of James can take this opportunity to encourage self-reflection. James 4:3 challenges the hearer to ask questions like:

What are my wants and desires?
How do I respond when I do not get what I want?
Are my desires characterised by selfishness or ambition?
Am I prioritising my own pleasure and comfort over the needs of others?

James teaches here that God is the one to grant a request. Earlier in the epistle, James described another scenario where one's request from God is denied: asking for wisdom while being divided in loyalty (1:6–8). Just like the duplicitous person does not receive anything from God, the one with selfish desires should not expect to receive their request.[23] James's repeated

23 Tamez refers to 1:6 and 4:3 as 'erroneous kinds of prayer'. See *Scandalous Message*, 57.

exhortations to care for the less fortunate (1:27; 2:5–7, 15–16; 5:1–6), insist that selfish gain shows duplicity.

## *2. Being an enemy of God and its remedy • James 4:4–10*

James's intensity reaches boiling point here in 4:4. In his condemnation of fights and selfishness, James resorts to calling his hearers by a shocking epithet: *adulteresses*. While the NIV renders this address as 'adulterous people', the term is feminine, particularly describing women unfaithful to their husbands. This name-calling is strong language; the shameful label is a sudden change from James's common address of 'brothers and sisters'.

Many in the modern West would be alarmed to receive such jarring words from their pastor. But James uses a disgraceful label to shock his hearers into paying attention. He is calling them to change their ways, as we will see later. James's approach is similar to the way many Asian parents place shameful labels on their children, calling them 'useless' or 'lazy'. While this sort of language might not be acceptable in many Western cultures, we must recognise its intent. Rather than using the labels with a spiteful intent – like the cursing in 3:9 – parents use this language to motivate children to change their ways. Likewise, James's strong language is used for his hearers' best interest, urging them to change their posture and direction.

While one might wonder if James is addressing actual adulterous sexual actions,[24] this saying is probably consistent with the biblical usage of adultery as a metaphor. It would be familiar to James's Jewish audience, as the prophets and Jesus used the imagery of adultery in castigating the people for their unfaithfulness to God (for example, Hosea 1–3; Jeremiah 13:27; Isaiah 1:21; Ezekiel

24 For this minority view, see F. J. A. Hort, *The Epistle of St. James* (London: MacMillan, 1909), 91–2.

16:32–8; Matthew 12:39).[25] James's label of 'adulteresses', then, bolsters his point that their selfishness and quarrels show them to be in rebellion against God. In *The Message*, Eugene Peterson's rendering of Hosea 1:2 captures the imagery's shock value for modern hearers: 'This whole country has become a whorehouse, unfaithful to me, GOD.'[26] Like adulteresses, James's hearers are more interested in indulging their desires than being faithful.

The adulterous behaviour is likened to aligning with the ways of the world. James uses parallel statements in communicating his point:

| | |
|---|---|
| . . . friendship with the world | means enmity against God |
| . . . friend of the world | becomes an enemy of God |

While the first line uses abstract terms, the new words of the second line and the conjunction 'therefore' take a step forward to make things personal: one can become 'an enemy of God'. Spiritual adultery, then, is much worse than physical adultery.

Much like in the address 'adulteresses', James's content goes beyond what the readers *do*; he writes about what they *are*. This resonates with much of the Global East, which is characterised by honour and shame. While those in guilt-based cultures might say, 'I made a mistake,' those in honour-based cultures would say, 'I *am* a mistake.'[27] James states that following the world does not just create enmity with God; they themselves *become enemies*.

What does James mean by the 'world' here? While 'world' sometimes carries a neutral sense of the inhabited realm (such as in James 2:5 and John 3:16), here James uses it in a negative

---

25 Allison suggests that James's words especially recall Hosea in James 4:4. See *James*, 606.

26 Eugene Peterson, *The Message: The Bible in Contemporary Language* (Colorado Springs: NavPress, 2002), 1609.

27 Georges and Baker, *Ministering in Honor-Shame Cultures*, 38.

sense, pitting it against God. The 'world' is the realm of rebellion against God. John wrote that one cannot love the world and God at the same time (1 John 2:15). Earlier, James had stated that religion acceptable before God is keeping 'oneself from being polluted by the world' (1:27).

In James 4:4, our author presents a dilemma of loyalty. While modern readers might use 'friend' to refer to acquaintances with whom we are friendly, 'friend' in the ancient world connoted allegiance. Indeed, Jesus declared to his disciples, 'You are my friends if you do what I command' (John 15:14). The Jewish leaders, shouting at Pilate with Jesus on trial, appealed to the requirement of allegiance: 'If you let this man go, you are no friend of Caesar. Anyone who claims to be a king opposes Caesar' (John 19:12).[28]

James's teaching echoes Jesus's words in the Sermon on the Mount: 'No one can serve two masters' (Matthew 6:24).[29] There is no middle ground. Like much of the epistle, James presents a binary choice: choose God or choose the world. Israel's heritage was characterised by the binary choice to choose the Lord rather than other gods (for example, Joshua 24:15; 1 Kings 18:21). Abraham chose the Lord, and James states that he was called a friend of God (2:23).

As we have discussed concerning James 2:1–7, the marginalised diaspora hearers of James might be tempted to align with the worldly rich to gain influence. Their situation is much like that of modern Christians in Asia. The poor in these cultures often depend on wealthy benefactors to meet their needs, entering into

---

28 The elements of allegiance and subordination would fit with the custom of patronage here, as the term 'friend' (*philos*) commonly referred to clients. For more, see the commentary at James 2:2–4, and my article, 'I Call You Friends'.

29 For a discussion about the possible traditions connected to James 4:4, including the saying of Jesus and early Christian literature, see Batten, *Friendship*, 158–65.

patron–client relationships.[30] James's message rings with modern relevance: do not align with the world, which is enmity with God.

James teaches that one cannot have both the world and God. There is an often-told fable about a peanut-loving monkey. One day, the monkey sees a bottle with a peanut inside. He scurries over to thrust his hand into the bottle. But as he closes his hand over the peanut, he finds that he is unable to pull out his fist. He is trapped. All the monkey must do is let go of the peanut, and he can be free. But as the story goes, he refuses to let go and tragically starves to death. The monkey cannot have both his freedom and the peanut. Similarly, the hearers of James cannot have both the world and God. They must choose the better of the two.

In addressing 'anyone who chooses', James states that enemies of God are responsible for their choices. We cannot blame others for our rebellion. Even here, James's repeated motif of judgment stands in the background – those who choose the world are deemed to be God's enemies. In the Old Testament, the binary choice between choosing God or others is often paired with the declaration that the Lord is jealous and punishes those who forsake him (Exodus 20:5; Joshua 24:19–20).

It is fitting that rebellion against God is portrayed as adultery. Adhering to God is not a one-time decision. People who are married make decisions every day to be devoted and committed to their spouse. Married people continuously provide food and shelter, emotional support and physical intimacy for each other. In the same way, faithfulness to God involves continuous resolve. Day-to-day decisions, from what to prioritise to the company we keep, define the lives of Christ-followers.

The association of a binary choice of whom to worship with God being jealous is furthered in James 4:5–6. This saying is difficult to decipher, as there is no known source for the statement

30 Cheung and Spurgeon, *James*, 85.

in 4:5b.[31] It is most sensible to start with the clearest element first: James 4:6b is a quotation of Proverbs 3:34. If we set aside the verse divisions – which are not original to the text – there is parallelism between the two sayings in 4:5–6:

| He jealously longs for the spirit he has caused to dwell in us | God opposes the proud |
|---|---|
| but he gives more grace. | and shows favour to the humble.[32] |

With this parallelism in view, the phrase 'Scripture says' in James 4:5a is probably referring to the quotation of Proverbs 3:34 in James 4:6b. Then, the first of the two parallel statements (4:5b–6a) is not necessarily a quotation of another text, but an exposition of the quotation to follow.[33]

The context of James 4:5–6 also informs our interpretation here. Given the association of the binary choice found in 4:4 with the Old Testament tradition of God being a jealous God, the term 'jealously' in 4:5 likely refers to God, which would suggest

---

31 There are more intertwined difficulties with James 4:5–6a. First, it is unclear whether the 'spirit' is the human spirit or the Holy Spirit. Second, 'spirit' could be the subject or object of the verb. Third, the phrase translated 'jealously' is difficult to interpret. For some proposals, see Sophie S. Laws, 'Does Scripture Speak in Vain? A Reconsideration of James IV. 5', *New Testament Studies* 20 (1974): 210–15; Richard Bauckham, 'The Spirit of God in Us Loathes Envy (James 4:5)', in Richard Bauckham, *The Jewish World Around the New Testament: Collected Essays I* (Tübingen: Mohr Siebeck, 2008), 421–32.

32 The Greek phrases rendered 'gives . . . grace' and 'shows favour' are identical.

33 This is the view of McKnight and Craig B. Carpenter, though they come to different conclusions about the details of this passage. See McKnight, *Letter of James*, 335–43; Craig B. Carpenter, 'James 4.5 Reconsidered', *New Testament Studies* 47 (2001): 189–205. I also commend the work of Douglas S. Huffman, 'James 4:5–6 and a Difficult to Locate OT Citation' (Annual Meeting of the Evangelical Theological Society, Denver, CO, 2022).

that the 'spirit' is the human spirit, as the NIV indicates.[34] God's jealousy, then, would refer to his rightful claim on the human spirit, against which the claims of proud speak. Indeed, 'enmity' and 'enemy' in 4:4 is echoed in 'opposed' in the quotation.

The modern teacher or preacher would be prudent not to dwell on deciphering the possible source or other details surrounding James 4:5. Rather, it would be wise to focus on the main point, which is clear: those who insist on fulfilling their selfish desires, resulting in fighting with others, have enmity towards God. With the quotation in 4:6, the hearers' problem is affirmed. They are God's enemies, as Paul also writes (Colossians 1:21; Romans 5:10). God is directly against them as if on the opposing side in a war. Their unfaithfulness, like that of Old Testament Israel, makes God jealous, and he is at odds with them. With selfishness expressed in their fights (4:1–3), they are double-minded and unstable (1:8), wavering in their commitment (1:6) and engaging in adultery against their master. James's indictment is palpable. They are in a wretched position!

But in spite of all the bad news, all is not lost. James presents good news to his hearers. The final clause of each of the two sayings in James 4:5–6 shows that God gives grace. Including himself in the recipients, James writes, 'he gives us more grace', and uses the same term for 'grace' in God 'shows favour to the humble'.

What is the grace – or gift – to which James refers? Differing interpretations consider it to be the Holy Spirit's help to overcome the evil desires, or the power to give God undivided allegiance. With the context of the passage in 4:7–9, 'grace' could also refer to the opportunity to become humble, to resist the enemy and to receive forgiveness.[35] But there is also the

34 So also Moo, *The Letter of James*, 239; Blomberg and Kamell, *James*, 191.

35 For different views, see Davids, *Epistle of James*, 164; McKnight, *Letter of James*, 342.

possibility that the 'grace' refers to eschatological reward, which is a recurring theme in this letter, especially with the saying in 4:10 in view. Considering the thesis statement of 1:12, it appears likely that James has in mind all the above. The hearers can repent, express allegiance to God alone, receive forgiveness and look forward to the final reward: all of this is a gift. We will discuss these elements in the treatment of 4:7–10.

James has the highest rate of imperative forms of any New Testament document,[36] and 4:7–10 contains the highest concentration within James. There are ten commands in rapid-fire succession, giving James's diaspora hearers the way to remedy their enmity with God. The conjunction 'then' (sometimes 'therefore') towards the beginning of 4:7 makes an inference in response to the quotation of Proverbs 3:34. In light of God's grace to the humble, James gives a detailed 'exhortation to *be* humble'.[37]

The first and last commands of James 4:7–10 are parallel, creating an *inclusio* to group the intervening sayings together.[38] The call to submit, which as Blomberg and Kamell say is a 'loaded term in our culture',[39] is the act of voluntarily placing ourselves under God's authority. If James is continuing the war imagery, the hearers must choose the side of God, then get into their proper rank and submit to their general.[40] Just like the 'show me' sayings in James 2:18 and 3:13, the willingness to be subjected shows one's allegiance to God to be genuine. Indeed, the former slave trader John Newton wrote that humility is one of 'the brightest evidences that He is indeed our Master'.[41]

---

36 See Varner's analysis in *James*, 22.

37 Vlachos, *James*, 142.

38 Both are passive in form, plural and have God/the Lord as the recipient. Martin sees it as an *inclusio*. See *James*, 152.

39 Blomberg and Kamell, *James*, 193.

40 Wiersbe, *Be Mature*, 132.

41 John Newton, *Cardiphonia: Or, the Utterance of the Heart; in the Course of a Real Correspondence* (London: Morgan & Scott, 1911), 277.

Societal values today resist any kind of external authority, urging individuals to 'be yourself' and 'live your truth'. The notion that individuals get to define good and evil for themselves seems fresh and novel, as if we are breaking free of age-old shackles. But this belief is not new. Nietzsche wrote *Beyond Good and Evil* to free people from traditional morality in the nineteenth century. Even so, his sentiment at the time was not new. The apostle Paul taught the connection between hostility towards God and not submitting to him: 'The mind governed by the flesh is hostile to God; it does not submit to God's law' (Romans 8:7). We see the period of the Judges characterised by people defining morality: 'everyone did as they saw fit' (Judges 17:6; 21:25). In fact, it was thousands of years ago that the serpent in the Garden enticed humans with defining good and evil on their own.

In the face of the human desire to define one's moral standard and be our own authority, James calls his hearers to submit to God. Like a soldier operating under a commanding officer or a regent carrying out the orders of a king, submission is voluntarily subordinating to God's will. We are to imitate the Lord Jesus, who called himself 'humble' (Matthew 11:29). We recall his prayer before his death asking for the cup to be removed, but declaring, 'Yet not my will, but yours be done' (Luke 22:42).

As part of being humble, James then exhorts his hearers to oppose the evil one: 'Resist the devil, and he will flee from you.' In contrast to God, the devil desires that people sin (1:13). While the source of the sin is human evil desire (1:14; 4:1), the devil is the one who tempts. Again, the binary choice is laid out: instead of choosing the world and being an enemy of God, the hearers of James are to choose submission to God and being the enemy of the devil.

The devil indeed opposes God and his people. 1 Peter 5, which also quotes Proverbs 3:34 in a call to be humble before

God, identifies the devil as the 'enemy' (1 Peter 5:8–10).[42] The devil is a roaring lion seeking to devour believers by inducing them into apostasy.[43] The apostle's exhortation is to 'resist him, standing firm in the faith' (1 Peter 5:9).

While James does not elaborate on resisting the devil, we can look to the apostle Paul, who urges Christ-followers to 'take your stand against the devil's schemes' in Ephesians 6:10–20. In the war against the enemy, followers of Christ can put on the full armour of God, which John Stott explains this way:

| | |
|---|---|
| • Belt of truth | Scripture to dispel the devil's lies |
| • Breastplate of righteousness | Pardon for sins and moral integrity |
| • Shoes of readiness of the gospel | The gospel frees people from the devil's tyranny |
| • Shield of faith | God's promises in times of doubt and temptation |
| • Helmet of salvation | Assurance of forgiveness and final deliverance |
| • Sword of the Spirit (the word of God) | Scripture for defence and resisting temptation[44] |

James's call to resist the devil is appropriately tied to being humble and submitting to God. While our Lord Jesus displayed humility, the devil exemplifies pride. C. S. Lewis wrote, 'It was through Pride that the devil became the devil.'[45] It is the proud

---

42 The verb 'resist' (*antistēte*) is identical in James 4:7 and 1 Peter 5:9.

43 Thomas R. Schreiner, *1–2 Peter and Jude* (Nashville: Holman Reference, 2020), 280.

44 John Stott, *The Message of Ephesians* (Downers Grove: IVP Academic, 1979), 275–83.

45 C. S. Lewis, *Mere Christianity* (New York: HarperOne, 2009), 122.

that God opposes (James 4:6). Resisting the devil places us on the side of God in this war.

James tells his hearers what will happen when they resist the devil: 'he will flee from you.' It is not merely quickly escaping, but taking flight *away*.[46] When encountering someone who aligns with God and actively resists, the devil will run away.

To be sure, the devil may not flee right away. The devil continues to be in battle with Christ's followers. It may take continued resistance, as Daniel Doriani says:

> Temptations fade slowly. Suppose a physician determines that a certain beloved spice (salt) or food (chocolate) is damaging his patient's health . . . To eat chocolate would be sin. But the desire for chocolate or salt is strong. The patient may have to resist the temptation over and over until the desire for that taste slowly fades away. So the devil flees, but perhaps not at once.[47]

The devil's fearful fleeing of a resisting Christian is warranted. Christ has already defeated the powers of evil, and believers can approach the war as victors. Believers, then, are not called to attack, but to defend ourselves. Note that equipment in the armour of God is mostly defensive. These pieces assist the saints in standing firm in the position that Christ has already won for us.[48] By holding on to God's promises and submitting to his will, Christ-followers will have victory.

While the devil flees, the hearers of James are to 'come near to God' (4:8) The theme of distance is stark in the contrast between the two sides of the war. Here, James echoes a concept familiar

46 In the LXX, 'flee' is used for Jonah's action in fleeing to Tarshish from the presence of the LORD (Jonah 1:3).

47 Daniel M. Doriani, *James* (Phillipsburg, NJ: P&R, 2007), 149.

48 Ernest Best, *Ephesians* (Edinburgh: Bloomsbury T&T Clark, 2004), 588.

to his diaspora hearers – the Old Testament motif of *nearness to God*. For example, the priests, after consecration, could 'approach the LORD' (Exodus 19:22), and bringing an offering involved coming near (Leviticus 21:21). To the people in exile because of their unfaithfulness, the Lord spoke through the prophets to instruct the people to turn from their ways: 'Return to me . . . and I will return to you' (Zechariah 1:3; see also Malachi 3:7). Here, James urges his hearers to have their fellowship with God restored. Indeed, closeness to God is a gift associated with blessedness. The author of Hebrews writes that we can approach God so that we will receive mercy and grace (Hebrews 4:16).

Like the previous command, James pairs his exhortation with a promise. This time, it echoes the prophetic literature: 'he will come near to you'. James's hearers, who have caused division and strife within their community, can restore the peace and be closer to God. The promise that God will 'come near' echoes the principle in James 4:6, that God gives grace to the humble. Even though they have committed adultery against God with their friendship with the world, James shows that the Lord 'woos his faithless wife', as Doriani puts it.[49]

The promise of being near to God would be especially meaningful to those in honour-based cultures. For the people, being near God was a mark of esteem. God was said to be 'near' to Israel (Deuteronomy 4:7), and the Lord dwelled with his people (Exodus 29:45). Conversely, being far from God is a disgrace. It is exemplified in Genesis 3:8, as the man and woman hid from the Lord because of their shame.

The diaspora hearers are keenly reminded of the disgrace of the Exile. The designation 'scattered among the nations' (1:1) is a painful reminder that the people are not near their homeland. Being far from their ancestral homeland, the hearers of James are unable to be near the physical centre of their ancestral

---

49 Doriani, *James*, 136.

culture. They probably experience the shame of being 'bad Jews', constantly encountering the tension between the customs and values of their new home and the ways of their heritage.

In writing this commentary, I am reminded that my lived experience resonates with that of these diaspora hearers of James. As a descendant of immigrants, I am constantly reminded that I am different from the majority culture. While I might dress and speak like those around me, I retain many of the customs and values of my ancestral culture. Even so, when I am among the immigrants who have retained even more of these ways, I feel shame. I experience the stigma of not keeping the traditions or not knowing the language well enough. In a number of ways, I am in the diaspora, a liminal space.[50]

In addition to being far from the centre of their culture, the hearers of James are far from the centre of their faith. They are unable to be near Jerusalem and the Temple. The Exile occurred because of their ancestors' rebellion, but they, too, are being indicted for their sins. They are called 'adulteresses' and 'enemies' of God (4:4). In other words, the hearers of James experience double degradation: for (a) being in the diaspora and (b) their own rebellion against God.

Amid their dishonour, the diaspora hearers receive an astounding offer. Not only can they receive grace if they humble themselves, but they are also able to be *near to God*. Even with their distance from Jerusalem, they can have relational closeness. The Lord had assured their ancestors that he would return to them. For the diaspora Jews following Christ, this promise is kept. They could experience the restored honour of being a people near to God. With their experience of unbelonging in both their home societies and their ancestral culture, they can belong. They can have a seat at God's table.

Jesus's parable of the prodigal son echoes some of the concepts

50 For more, see my 'Asian Reflections on James'.

found in James 4:8a. The younger son, in his disgraceful action against his father, is in a 'distant country' (Luke 15:13) – with the stigma of being 'far' from his people and 'far' from relationship with his father. When he returns home, his father sees him 'far' off and runs to come near to him. The younger son is restored to his honoured position in the family, and – most importantly – to his relationship with his father.[51] Likewise, James teaches that those who humble themselves can be restored to God, and God will draw near to them.

Next, James continues calling for his hearers to be humble and to submit to God, with parallel sayings in 4:8b:

| | |
|---|---|
| Wash your hands | you sinners |
| Purify your hearts | you double-minded |

The two sayings draw on the hearers' familiarity with the Old Testament motif of associating cleanliness with righteousness. The imagery of washing hands and hearts (see also Jeremiah 4:14; Job 22:30) is exemplified in Psalm 24:3–4:

> Who may ascend the mountain of the LORD?
> Who may stand in his holy place?
> The one who has clean hands and a pure heart,
> who does not trust in an idol
> or swear by a false god.

With this concept of purity, James continues a biblical motif of sin as moral filth, which he introduced in 1:21 and 1:27.[52]

In 'sinners' and 'double-minded', James again departs from his

---

51 For an analysis of the parable's honour-based elements, see Daniel K. Eng, 'The Widening Circle: Honour, Shame, and Collectivism in the Parable of the Prodigal Son', *The Expository Times* 130, no. 5 (2019): 193–201.

52 In Hebrews 10:22, the author also associates drawing near with cleanliness.

familiar address of 'brothers and sisters'. Much like 'adulteresses', the two new addresses in quick succession are emphatic,[53] as James calls them to change their ways and turn back to God. They are called to see a problem in themselves that needs a drastic remedy. The address 'double-minded' is especially poignant, as it describes the condemned person with wavering loyalties in 1:8. The hearers are called to turn from their doubleness – their duplicity – and be singly submitted to God.

Submitting to God requires intentionality. It cannot be achieved passively. I sometimes observe that our family minivan, when left out in the rain, doesn't get any cleaner. Rather, it requires some intentionality – some purposeful scrubbing – to be rid of filth. In the same way, James urges his hearers to actively address their sin and turn from it.

With the appeal to the hands and the heart, James's 'show me' motif returns here – the call to change is not just on the inside. Drawing near to God is a total change, requiring both obedient action and humble disposition.[54] This is the concept of repentance – the intentional turning from sin and committing to change. Chuck Colson recalls the infamous American gangster Mickey Cohen, who responded to an invitation from a visiting Christian leader for conversion. But as months passed, people did not observe any change; he had not left his life of organised crime. When confronted about it, he responded that 'no one had told him he would have to give up his work or his friends'.[55] Unlike Cohen's false repentance, true repentance is a total work of both the heart and the hands. Change must be observable.

---

53 See 'Changed Reference' in Runge, *Discourse Grammar*, 354–63.

54 Scot McKnight, *Galatians*, The NIV Application Commentary (Grand Rapids: Zondervan, 1995), 350.

55 Charles Colson, *Who Speaks for God? Confronting the World with Real Christianity* (Westchester, IL: Good News Publications, 1985), 153.

While repentance can seem to be a tall order, this cleansing is a cooperation between people and God. In his psalm of repentance after committing adultery with Bathsheba, David pleads with God to 'create in me a pure heart' (Psalm 51:10). The apostle John declares that Jesus's blood purifies us from sin, and we must confess and be cleansed (1 John 1:7, 9). Augustine prayed, 'Grant what Thou dost command and command what Thou wilt.'[56]

James continues his call for submission to God with several related commands in 4:9: 'Grieve, mourn and wail,' and, 'Change your laughter to mourning and your joy to gloom.' This, too, echoes a biblical motif that the revelation of sin leads to sorrow (see Nehemiah 8:9; Jeremiah 9:19; 1 Corinthians 5:2).

Mourning is appropriate in expectation of God's judgment. James repeatedly appeals to end-time judgment, explicitly discussing its imminence in 5:8. Like the Lord called the exiles to return to him with weeping and mourning (Joel 2:12), James calls his hearers to mourn now. This is for their good; as Moo says, 'They can wait to mourn until it is too late, when God has brought his judgment on the earth. Or they can mourn now, turning sorrowfully from their sin.'[57] Repentance in this life will turn into a favourable state in the end, as Jesus preached in the Sermon on the Mount: 'Blessed are those who mourn, for they will be comforted' (Matthew 5:4). It is not too late.

With 'Change your laughter to mourning and your joy to gloom,' James reminds his hearers that the situation is grave. Like a parent scolding a child to 'wipe that smile off your face' to show penitence, the hearers are not to take this lightly. Recalling the great reversal in James 1:9–11, those who are humble now will be exalted later, and those who are exalted now will be

56 Augustine of Hippo, *Confessions*, ed. Roy Joseph Deferrari, trans. Vernon J. Bourke (Washington, DC: Catholic University of America Press, 1953), 298.
57 Moo, *The Letter of James*, 247.

humiliated later. Jesus declared, 'Woe to you who laugh now, for you will mourn and weep' (Luke 6:25). His followers should never take sin lightly.

Mourning may appear to contradict James's exhortation to have joy (1:2) or Paul's command to 'rejoice in the Lord always' (Philippians 4:4). But both James's and Paul's commands for joy are rooted in God's work in the believer – the process of being mature and complete and the forgiveness we receive in Christ.[58] Here in James 4:9, the condemned laughter comes from flippant hope in the temporal, earthly life.

The teacher of James should make no mistake: repentance itself does not wash away sins. It is the death of Christ on the cross that makes atonement. However, the Lord requires contrition and commitment to change. Indeed, as James continues the 'show me' motif, mourning over sins shows one's commitment to God. As the nineteenth-century Bishop J. C. Ryle stated, 'Justified people are always penitent people, and . . . a forgiven sinner will always be a man who mourns over, and loathes his sins.'[59]

In James 4:10, our author sums up the subsection by returning to the concept of humility introduced in 4:7. After the many commands in 4:7–10a, he gives a promise: 'he will lift you up.' This saying recalls the prologue: the believers – humbled – will have a high position (1:9) and receive the crown of life (1:12). The exaltation, then, does not occur in this life, but in the end. Indeed, by humbling themselves, they will receive the 'grace' and 'favour' described in 4:5–6.

The end of the letter's body in 4:10 is a fitting place for the command to be humble, since this theme has been occurring throughout the letter. The call to be humble recalls the quotation of Proverbs 3:34. Since God gives grace to the humble, the way to receive this grace is to humble ourselves.

---

58 Moo compares James 4:9 with Philippians 4:4.

59 J. C. Ryle, *Old Paths* (London: W. Hunt, 1878), 411.

The call to humility also connects to James's discussion of God's favour on the poor. The hearers have already received the message that the lowly will be exalted in eternity (1:9) and that the poor who love God will receive eternal inheritance (2:5). Being humble before God is to recognise one's spiritual poverty. Just like the materially poor have lowly status and must depend on others, followers of Christ must humbly express their stark need to depend on God.[60] It is in this spirit that Jesus himself teaches in the Sermon on the Mount, 'Blessed are the poor in spirit, for theirs is the kingdom of heaven' (Matthew 5:3).

The humbling that James describes comes 'before the Lord'. After all, it is unlikely that we become humble by looking at other people. We see this in the home when a parent scolds a child for having a messy room, and the child gives the excuse, 'You think my room is bad, you should see . . .' and points at a messier child.[61] We recall Jesus's parable of the Pharisee and the tax collector, in which the former compares himself not to God, but to robbers, evildoers and adulterers (Luke 18:11). This pride sets one at odds with God; C. S. Lewis fittingly calls pride 'the complete anti-God state of mind'.[62]

However, James's teaching is to view ourselves in relation to the Holy One – the true standard. Author David Brooks calls humility 'having an accurate assessment of your own nature and your own place in the cosmos'.[63] We understand our place in the cosmos with 'death to self' and the 'enthronement of God'.[64] This is exemplified by the tax collector's dependence on the Lord: 'God, have mercy on me, a sinner.' It is this humble man, according to Jesus, who is 'justified before God' (Luke 18:13–14).

60 Moo, *The Letter of James*, 248.

61 Doriani, *James*, 151.

62 Lewis, *Mere Christianity*, 122.

63 David Brooks, *The Road to Character* (New York: Random House, 2015), 263.

64 Andrew Murray, *Humility: The Beauty of Holiness* (New York: Fleming H. Revell, 1800), 73, 59.

Just like the promise of God coming near, the promise of being lifted up is particularly significant to James's hearers. As James shows in the Canaanite prostitute Rahab having the same status as the celebrated patriarch Abraham, God has a predilection for the outcast.[65] There is no favouritism with God (2:1–9); even those marginalised in society can be lifted up. Being minorities in the diaspora, they are probably discriminated against both for being Jewish and for being Christian. Like modern minorities, they have limited resources and limited influence. Amid their earthly difficulties (see 1:2), they can place their hope in end-time exaltation.

African American spirituals, set in the context of slavery, often embodied a message of hope similar to the one James pronounces to his underprivileged hearers. During difficult circumstances, these songs became profound reminders that God would indeed reward those who are faithful to him:

> There'll be singing, there'll be singing,
> there'll be singing over me.
> And before I'd be a slave
> I'll be buried in my grave,
> and go home to my Lord and be free.[66]

Freedom from difficulty may not come in this life, but there is hope for those enduring trial that God will lift them up in the end.

While James's indictment is at a boiling point in 4:4, here in 4:10 the good news reaches a crescendo. The teacher or preacher of James can focus the audience's attention on the good news here. After establishing the terrible position of his hearers being enemies of God in 4:1–3, James gives this joyous message: there

65 See Tamez, *Scandalous Message*, 35.
66 'Oh Freedom', public domain.

is hope in God's grace. There is a solution provided by God, epitomised by the epistle's thesis in 1:12. In this way, James echoes Jesus's words in the Sermon on the Mount: 'Blessed are the meek, for they will inherit the earth' (Matthew 5:5). As in the rest of the Beatitudes, for those who exhibit the affirmed behaviour, a blessed state will be realised in the life to come. By becoming humbled before God, they can place their hope in eternal reward.

## *3. Summarising transition: slander and judgment • James 4:11–12*

James 4:11–12 can be difficult to place with the surrounding text.[67] Some group James 4:11–12 with 4:1–10, connecting 'slander' with the strife and worldliness in 4:1–4 and the affirmation of God as the only judge (4:12) to whom we submit (4:7).[68] Others associate 4:11–12 with the content following it, with 4:11–12, 13–17 and 5:1–6 as examples of arrogance that the Lord opposes (4:6).[69]

The teacher of James should not miss that James 4:11–12 sums up the epistle's content. It not only relates to the content immediately preceding it, but also connects to even earlier portions of the letter.[70] The warnings against slander echo the calls to proper speech ethics (1:19, 26; 3:1–12). The affirmation of God as the Lawgiver (see Isaiah 33:22) recalls the exhortations to persevere and fulfil the law (1:25; 2:8). The appeal to judgment reminds the hearers to act in expectation of future judgment (2:12–13; 3:1). Finally, the condemnation of slandering recalls their cursing and quarrels (3:9–10; 4:1–2).

---

67 I give a detailed treatment in Eng, *Eschatological Approval*, 83–6.

68 See, for example, Blomberg and Kamell, *James*, 196–7; Dibelius, *James*, 228.

69 Robert W. Wall, *Community of the Wise: The Letter of James* (Valley Forge, PA: Trinity, 1997), 210–13; Cheung and Spurgeon, *James*, 89–99.

70 Davids observes that 4:11–12 reaches back to 3:9–12 in discussing community conflict. See Davids, *Epistle of James*, 168–9.

As discussed above, James 4:11–12 pairs with 2:12–13 to create an *inclusio*. The clustering of terms about (a) speaking, (b) acting in relation to the law, and (c) judgment marks the opening and closing of the body of James.

In addition to being a summary, these sayings in James 4:11–12 preview the content following it. In addition to the aforementioned connections with 4:13–17 and 5:1–6, the connections continue beyond 5:6. James will return to the familiar address of 'brothers and sisters' in 5:7 after the interlude (see below) of 4:13–5:6. Also, the epistle's repeated appeals to judgment, which appear again in 4:11–12, return in 5:9 and 5:12. Furthermore, the discussion of behaviour that impacts 'one another' (4:11) in the hearers' community is picked up in 5:9 and 5:16.

For the modern teacher of the book of James, 4:11–12 can be grouped with 4:1–10, which keeps the teaching units similar in length. This arrangement can fit well, as these sayings serve to conclude the epistle's main body. Also, this is an appropriate place in the epistle for a summarising transition, as we will see that 4:13–17 and 5:1–6 address an audience outside the epistle's hearers.

Here, James returns to the familial address of 'brothers and sisters'. After the jarring labels of 'adulteresses', 'sinners' and 'double-minded', the message of hope in 4:10 communicates that James has not given up on his hearers.[71] With this familiar address, James brings attention to the command, 'Do not slander one another.'

In this revisiting of speech ethics, James condemns the use of the tongue against others. As mentioned above, this could be an extension of the cursing found in 3:9–10 and the 'quarrels' that were causing divisions in 4:1–3. The verb occurs three times in 4:11, rendered as 'slander' (once) and 'speaks against' (twice). The same term also occurs in 1 Peter 2:12 and 3:16, both

71 McCartney, *James*, 220.

times referring to outsiders maliciously speaking false accusations against the behaviour of Peter's hearers. Much like its usage in 1 Peter, the rest of the content in James 4:11 points to this slander and speaking against someone as setting up the speaker as the judge. James equates the act of speaking against someone with speaking against the law and judging the law.

Several questions arise with the sayings in James 4:11. What 'law' is James discussing? How does this act of speaking against someone become judging the law? What counts as slander? Shouldn't those in the church warn others about their sin?

Since the sayings in James 4:11–12 form a unit of thought, we ought to view them in relation to one another. The final saying can provide a way forward.[72] Rather than his usual 'brother or sister' (just used in 4:11), James uses the term 'neighbour'. For his diaspora audience, James is likely evoking the command to 'love your neighbour as yourself', found in Leviticus 19:18. The aforementioned connection between 4:11–12 and 2:12–13, the latter of which comes in the context of this command (see 2:8), corroborates this association.[73] Furthermore, James's condemnation of speaking against or slandering someone recalls Leviticus 19:16: 'Do not go about spreading slander among your people.'

With the two commands in view, [74] James states that anyone who 'speaks against' a brother or sister is breaking the law to love one's neighbour. Clearly this speaking against is an action not done out of love. After all, James himself has been speaking against the sinful actions of his hearers, and doing so out of loving concern. Later, he will encourage them to bring back a person

72 Moo writes, 'Clearly a part of the argument is missing' and points to 'neighbour' at the end of these sayings as a starting point. See *The Letter of James*, 250.

73 For more on James's appeals to Leviticus 19, see Luke Timothy Johnson, 'The Use of Leviticus 19 in the Letter of James', *Journal of Biblical Literature* 101 (September 1982): 391–401.

74 Nystrom calls Leviticus 19:18 the 'clear' foil to the prohibition of slander. See *James*, 249.

if they 'wander from the truth' (5:19–20). Here, however, James puts speaking against or 'slander' at odds with loving someone.

We observe more about the nature of 'slander' from the content in James 4:11. The act of slandering is 'close cousins' with judging.[75] Thus, the contrast of these terms with loving one's neighbour shows that James is condemning a type of speaking based on its intention. This fits with James's 'inside-outside' motif. By slandering or speaking against someone, James has in mind the type of speech that sets a person up as a judge over another.

The motif of judgment comes up repeatedly in the epistle of James, affirming each time that judgment is done by God and condemning each time judgment is done by people. True to form, James reminds his hearers that 'there is only one Lawgiver and Judge'. The implication, of course, is clear: 'It's not you!' The act of slandering or speaking against a brother or sister, then, amounts to usurping the role of judge, which belongs to God alone.

Why does James equate speaking against or judging someone with speaking against or judging the law? With the term 'neighbour' in close proximity, 'law' most likely refers to the love commandment of Leviticus 19:18, the same one James called the 'royal law' in 2:8.[76] This commandment was foundational to the ethics of Israel, and Jesus affirmed the paramount nature of this command, calling it the 'second' great command (Matthew 22:39; also 19:19). The apostle Paul declared that the other commands are 'summed up in this one', and that 'whoever loves others has fulfilled the law' (Romans 13:8–9).

By breaking the love command while positioning oneself as a judge over others, the 'slanderer' thereby 'speaks against' the command, treating the law with contempt. The perpetrator is

---

75 McCartney, *James*, 220.

76 'Royal' could refer to the Lord as the King of Israel, or to Jesus as the King. See the commentary at 2:8.

judging it, standing over it and deeming it unworthy of following. In this way, one who 'speaks against' a brother or sister is elevating oneself above the law, usurping God's role as Lawgiver. As we will see in James 5:19–20, this person is standing over another person as the judge rather than standing side by side with a person, pointing to the only Judge.

One who slanders is not appealing to the standard of God, but is setting up a *human standard*. James has previously condemned those who use human standards, calling those who show favouritism to the rich 'judges with evil thoughts' (2:4). Temptations to judge others based on human standards are all too familiar. In my circles, churchgoers sometimes condemn others for using specific music styles in worship services. We in the church have denigrated particular genres of literature, or even watching films. Today, we denounce those who have differing political views, even those about which Scripture is silent. James's words here apply to the church in any era.

To be sure, the church is called to identify and point out the sinful actions of others in the church. Jesus taught, 'If your brother or sister sins, go and point out their fault' (Matthew 18:15). By doing so, one must judge, evaluate the action. Indeed, the apostle Paul wrote, 'What business is it of mine to judge those outside the church? Are you not to judge those inside? . . . "Expel the wicked person from among you"' (1 Corinthians 5:12–13). But when those in the church point out the sins of others, we must appeal to *God's standard*. In this way, when we do this out of love, we are fulfilling the love commandment by caring for the best interests of both the individual and the community.

To be sure, judging out of concern for someone is a fine line to walk. Even when done gently, pointing out someone else's sin is often received as a personal attack. One must be wise about how to approach this sort of loving confrontation. Furthermore, we ought to evaluate ourselves. It would be prudent to ask, 'Am I approaching someone with the right motivations?' Fittingly,

Paul writes, 'If someone is caught in a sin, you who live by the Spirit should restore that person gently. But watch yourselves, or you also may be tempted' (Galatians 6:1). If one discerns an inclination to denigrate or take authority over another, one may be setting themselves up as lawgiver and judge.

James reminds his hearers not only that God is the sole Lawgiver and Judge, but also that he is the 'one who is able to save and destroy'. The Lord gave the law, and he will be the one to judge all the people of the earth, standing, as McCartney says, 'at both the beginning and end of redemptive history'.[77] With God as the sole authority, the hearers are called to submit themselves to his will (4:7) as they expect him to judge (5:9). Ultimately, only God decides if someone is saved or destroyed.[78] Jesus taught his disciples not to fear human powers, but to 'be afraid of the One who can destroy both soul and body in hell' (Matthew 10:28).

With James 4:11–12, our author ends the main body of the epistle. These sayings sum up the calls to proper speech ethics, to perseverance in adherence to the law and to a life lived in expectation of imminent judgment. As we will see, these sayings also give a preview of the sections that conclude James.

---

77 McCartney, *James*, 221.

78 In the LXX, 'save' refers to eternal salvation when associated with God's judgment (for example, Isaiah 45:17–22; Ezekiel 34:22).

# 10

# Apostrophe

## JAMES 4:13–5:6

After James 4:11–12 closes the main body of the epistle, the author presents two sections that function as apostrophe, or the addressing of an absent party for the benefit of the actual hearers. The first section (4:13–17) addresses merchants, and the second (5:1–6) addresses the rich.

The modern teacher of James can approach these two passages as a single teaching unit, because they share several links. First, they are connected by the repeated opening of, 'Now listen,' (woodenly, 'Come now'). Second, both groups – the merchants and the rich – have significant financial means. Third, the descriptions of both groups focus on the attainment of wealth.[1]

Several cues indicate that James is likely addressing those outside the hearers of the epistle.[2] First, neither section contains James's common address, 'brothers and sisters'. The address does not return until after these two sections and occurs three times in 5:7–11. Also, the two sections do not contain 'of you' or 'among you' (see 3:1; 4:1; 5:13, 14, 19), which point to the communities of the hearers.

Second, both sections share a condemnatory tone, without an exhortation to repent. While the content within the *inclusio* of

---

1 Matthias Konradt, *Christliche Existenz nach dem Jakobusbrief: eine Studie zu seiner soteriologischen und ethischen Konzeption* (Göttingen: Vandenhoeck & Ruprecht, 1998), 159.

2 See my full treatment in Eng, *Eschatological Approval*, 86–8.

2:12–13 and 4:11–12 is marked by calls to remember judgment and to motivate the hearers to change, these sections pronounce woe on the two parties. They fit with a pattern of prophetic condemnation (such as in Isaiah 45:10; Habakkuk 2:15; Luke 6:24–6).[3] The merchants are said to vanish in 4:14, much like the rich 'fade away' in 1:11. The rich in 5:1 are called to 'wail' in the expectation of divine wrath when judgment comes.

Third, the tone of these passages is even more notable as we discern a shift back to the consolation of the hearers in 5:7–11.[4] Instead of the wrath of the Lord Almighty (5:4), James discusses the 'compassion and mercy' of the Lord (5:11) with the 'brothers and sisters'.

Fourth, neither section has exhortations using imperatives for the hearers to reform their behaviour. As James is the New Testament book with the highest percentage of imperatives,[5] having no imperative forms that call for repentance in 4:13–5:6 is a considerable anomaly.

With apostrophe, a speaker or author does not expect the addressees to hear. James, in addressing those outside his audience, uses a literary device that the Old Testament prophets employed.[6] While the message is not addressed *to* his audience, it is nonetheless *for* them.

## *1. Apostrophe A: arrogant merchants • James 4:13–17*

In James 4:13–17, James addresses those who travel to do business and make profit. We recall that James's diaspora hearers are disadvantaged; it would be unlikely that they have the means

3 See Maynard-Reid, *Poverty and Wealth*, 70–71.

4 McKnight calls the tone in 5:7–11 'a pastoral level'. See *Letter of James*, 402.

5 Varner, *James*, 22.

6 See, for example, Nahum 2; Jeremiah 49:15–16; Obadiah 1–18.

and influence to travel regularly. As discussed above, James has a message for his audience by feigning his address to a different party. The language of 'this or that city' makes clear that these merchants are fictional.[7]

*Boasting about tomorrow*

**13** Now listen, you who say, 'Today or tomorrow we will go to this or that city, spend a year there, carry on business and make money.' **14** Why, you do not even know what will happen tomorrow. What is your life? You are a mist that appears for a little while and then vanishes. **15** Instead, you ought to say, 'If it is the Lord's will, we will live and do this or that.' **16** As it is, you boast in your arrogant schemes. All such boasting is evil. **17** If anyone, then, knows the good they ought to do and doesn't do it, it is sin for them.

As stated in James 4:13, these merchants make plans for their travel, delineating their business and ensuring their profit. Here, James conveys that they are not humble before God, submitting to his will. In this, they are boasting, arrogant and guilty of sin.

James is not stating that engaging in business or making travel plans are sinful behaviours. The Scriptures affirm hard work and advance planning: 'The plans of the diligent lead to profit' (Proverbs 21:5). Jesus positively portrays someone making plans to build a tower (Luke 14:28) and making contingencies for the future (Luke 16:4). James would not condemn modern actions of planning, like saving up for a purchase or investing in retirement accounts.

Rather, James is condemning the merchants presuming on their future without submitting to God. The problem with their planning is their attitudes: they 'boast in [their] arrogant schemes' (4:16). The merchants assure themselves that they will 'make money' with their endeavours. They do not consider God's will (4:15), but deem themselves to be the determinants of what will happen.

7 Moo, *The Letter of James*, 255.

James's content here recalls descriptions of the wicked being arrogant and boasting in the Scriptures (such as Habakkuk 2:4; Psalm 10:3). The prophets especially condemn merchants who have a reputation for being corrupt and cheating the poor (Zephaniah 1:11; Hosea 12:7; Amos 8:4–6).

James declares to the merchants – reminding his actual hearers – that life is fleeting (4:14). By likening the merchants to a mist that vanishes, he issues a reminder that human beings are unlike God. Our fortunes could change, and we can depart at any moment. The imagery of mist vanishing recalls the rich who, like a wild flower, will pass away (1:10–11). James chides the merchants that they do not know what will happen tomorrow – their very lives could be gone. The merchants' boasting (4:16) defies the warning in Proverbs 27:1, 'Do not boast about tomorrow, for you do not know what a day may bring.'

I remember watching a tragic news report in 2021 about the twelve-storey building, Champlain Towers South in Surfside, Florida. At 1:22 a.m. on 24 June 2021, the beachfront condominium complex collapsed. With many of its residents inside at the time, ninety-eight people died. Without warning, our lives can end in the blink of an eye.

The merchants do not remember that their worldly status and their very lives are like a mist that can vanish at any time. James's words share several themes with a parable that Jesus told (Luke 12:16–20) of a man who, after an unexpectedly abundant harvest, makes plans to build bigger barns to store the grain and presumes that he will enjoy it for 'many years'. But an unexpected twist happens for the man: 'But God said to him, "You fool! This very night your life will be demanded from you. Then who will get what you have prepared for yourself?"'

In his indictment of the boasting merchants, James presents in 4:15 the alternative to arrogant planning: an attitude that would say, 'If it is the Lord's will, we will live and do this or that.' This is not an exhortation for the merchants to follow. As stated above, there is no imperative verb in this saying. One could translate the Greek text this way: 'Instead of your saying, "If the Lord wills, we will live . . .," you are now boasting.'[8] This logic would fit well with 4:17, which describes someone knowing the good they ought to do and not doing it. Even with the NIV's addition of 'you ought to say' in 4:17, it is not a command. James is not expecting the merchants to change their ways. Rather, he presents the contrast between an attitude that presumes the future and an attitude that submits the future to God.

I remember a mentor who made his default email signature 'd.v.' before his name. He put a clarifying note under it: 'd.v. = *deo volente*, God willing'. Through his regular emails, he reminded his recipients – and himself – that our future is determined by God. As Proverbs 16:9 teaches, 'In their hearts humans plan their course, but the LORD establishes their steps.' Through two letters at the end of his messages, my mentor reminded me to submit my plans to God.

A saying akin to 'if the Lord wills' is often called the *conditio Jacobaea* – the reservation of James. The 'condition' is not just a phrase to speak; it is to be accompanied by action. We are to recognise that the future is determined by God. This attitude serves to characterise those who follow Jesus. As he instructed in his model prayer (Matthew 6:10), Jesus himself prays 'your will be done' (Matthew 26:42).

Again, James here presents two ways to live. The merchants, as they presume with 'arrogant schemes', show the way of the world, which is opposed to God (4:4). Amid their 'evil' boasting, they end up vanishing. The hearers, however, can live the other way, submitting to God in humility (4:7, 10). They can embody the maxim in Proverbs 16:3, 'Commit to the LORD whatever you do, and he will establish your plans.'

Modern technology places each individual in quick control of

8 As proposed in McKnight, *Letter of James*, 374.

our plans. Many of us reach for our electronic devices first thing in the morning, as if much depends on us and our calendars. Perhaps we have opportunities to do good deeds, like care for a needy neighbour. But we think, 'I'll get to that later,' with the assumption that we are in control of our time. James reminds us that our illusion of control can lead us to arrogantly boast about our future. Like the merchants, we become functional atheists. We go through our lives as if God does not exist. Today, more than ever, we are called to humbly submit to the Lord's will.

Much like in previous sections (2:13, 26; 3:13), in 4:17 James concludes with a timeless truth: 'If anyone, then, knows the good they ought to do and doesn't do it, it is sin for them.' Unlike a sin of commission, which is a wilful act that violates a command, James refers to a sin of omission. It is a sin when one fails to do what is right.

I remember visiting a small town in the Netherlands that was home to a chocolate factory. As we walked around town, we could constantly smell the chocolate. But as we paid less attention to the factory, our senses adapted and we forgot about the smell. Sins of omission can be like our adapting sense of smell. Neglecting to adhere to the word of God, we can easily go about our lives and neglect God as well.

Sins of omission include not doing what God's word states (see 1:22–5). This could include ignoring the commands to care for the poor (2:16) or the failure to bridle the tongue (3:3–12). But in James 4:17, the 'sin' in question most naturally refers to the boasting that is evil in 4:16. While one can wonder if James's addressees, the merchants, know that such boasting is evil, the actual hearers of this epistle know; they are now being told. James conveys, through his apostrophe, that the hearers ought to be humble and trust in God. If they do not, they are committing a sin of omission.

## *2. Apostrophe B: wicked rich • James 5:1–6*

After addressing the arrogant merchants for the sake of his actual hearers, James now addresses another party: rich landowners who oppress and cheat their workers. Just like in James 4:13–17, it is unlikely that this party is hearing the words of this epistle. Rather, James is using the literary device of apostrophe – addressing those outside his audience – to convey a message to the actual hearers.

*Warning to rich oppressors*

**5** Now listen, you rich people, weep and wail because of the misery that is coming on you. **2** Your wealth has rotted, and moths have eaten your clothes. **3** Your gold and silver are corroded. Their corrosion will testify against you and eat your flesh like fire. You have hoarded wealth in the last days. **4** Look! The wages you failed to pay the workers who mowed your fields are crying out against you. The cries of the harvesters have reached the ears of the Lord Almighty. **5** You have lived on earth in luxury and self-indulgence. You have fattened yourselves in the day of slaughter.[a] **6** You have condemned and murdered the innocent one, who was not opposing you.

[a] 5 Or *yourselves as in a day of feasting*

Through the words of James, we observe references to social strata in the world of his hearers.[9] James distinguishes his hearers from the rich, the ones who are exploiting them and dragging them into court (2:6). Some 'brothers and sisters' among them are destitute, being without clothes and food (2:15). Others, however, can find work, serving as labourers to wealthy landowners. Here, for the sake of the hearers, James feigns an address to these landowners.

James starts this section by telling the rich to 'weep and

9 Tamez, *Scandalous Message*, 25.

wail'.[10] As discussed above in the introduction to 4:13–17, this is not a command to repent. Unlike the mourning associated with change in 4:9, this call speaks of the fate these rich people will face. For the sake of his hearers – the ones being exploited (2:6) – James pronounces this message of woe.

James 5:1–6 can be delineated this way:

| | |
|---|---|
| A Command | Weep and wail (5:1a) |
| B Grounds for A | Misery is coming, wealth is corroded (5:1b–3a) |
| C Testimony about B | Corrosion speaks of their guilt – they will suffer (5:3b) |
| D Justification for C | They have cheated their workers and lived in luxury at their expense, but the day of slaughter has arrived. They have murdered the innocent one (5:4–6). |

Each of the three parallel sayings in James 5:2–3a features an object of riches: wealth, clothes and precious metals. For each, James pronounces that they have lost their value; their riches are worthless. The first one, 'wealth', may encompass the second and third: garments and coins. The second, garments, is a visible indicator of status. Indeed, the 'fine clothes' of the man in 2:2 showed his wealth and influence. Over time, even the finest clothes can become moth-eaten; one recalls James's description of the 'fading away' of the rich (1:10–11) and Jesus's warning about the moth destroying earthly treasures (Matthew 6:19).

The third saying, describing gold and silver, is especially poignant. Since true gold and silver cannot corrode, the 'rust' indicates that the precious metals are false. As discussed above in the commentary at James 1:2–4, the author likely uses metallurgic

10 All the instances of 'you' in James 5:2–6 are plural.

testing imagery to describe his hearers' trials. If the hearers come out of the fiery testing like precious metals, they are approved by their evaluator (1:12). James is likely continuing this imagery in discussing rusty gold and silver.

In fact, the rust of their gold and silver will testify against them. The corrosion is not merely evidence; James personifies the rust, as if it were speaking. Here, another courtroom setting is conveyed, but not where the rich are exploiting others (2:6). Rather, the tables have turned; the rich are now on trial. They will face the true judge, and they will be indicted. The corrosion – evidence of false gold and silver – speaks to metalworker-judge. The rich will not be approved in the end-time judgment, but condemned.

What testifies against the rich is not gold and silver itself. If it were, we would be tempted to think that James is condemning wealth or the attainment of wealth. Just like planning for the future is not evil (see commentary for 4:13–17), wealth itself is not evil. We see wealthy figures who are faithful to the Lord, like Abraham and Boaz. Rather, the witness against the rich is the corrosion. An assayer, or evaluator of precious metals, would deem rusty metals as false gold and silver. Likewise, the judge declares the rich to be false; they are guilty.

Furthermore, the corrosion will eat the rich's flesh like fire. Like fire burns away the dross, or refuse metals, the rich are consumed just like false precious metals.[11] This is likely an echo of the prophetic literature that depicts God as a metalworker, removing the dross – the lawless and the sinners (see Isaiah 1:21–6; Jeremiah 6:27–30). For the rich, the fire does not refine them – they will not be tried and true (1:12). In an ironic twist, the rich are consumed by the corrosion along with their gold

11 Johnson suggests the connection with fire-tested gold as described in 1 Peter 1:7. See *Letter of James*, 300.

and silver.[12] Just like the very riches they hoarded, the rich will be no more.

The final clause in James 5:3, 'in the last days', indicates that the 'misery' (5:1) and the eating of the rich's flesh will occur in the end times. In the Old Testament, 'last days' refers to the era when the Lord brings a consummation of history (for example, Hosea 3:5; Isaiah 2:2; Micah 4:1). The New Testament uses 'last days' to describe the same period, which is inaugurated by Jesus (Acts 2:17; 2 Timothy 3:1; Hebrews 1:2).[13] Like the Old Testament prophets, by James's use of the perfect tense – 'has rotted', 'have eaten', 'are corroded' – he vividly communicates that the depreciation is as good as done.[14] In these last days, the time between the two 'comings' of Christ, it is the time to repent (see 4:7–10). But rather than repenting, the rich have hoarded wealth. Like the prophet Zephaniah declared, 'Neither their silver nor their gold will be able to save them on the day of the LORD's wrath' (Zephaniah 1:18). James does not convey any hope for the rich; they will receive their fiery punishment.

James gives justification for the rich's condemnation. First, in 5:4 he declares that their wealth is ill-gotten. They have kept fair wages from their labourers. Here, James personifies another inanimate object – the withheld wages themselves are crying out. The image recalls the blood of Abel crying out to the Lord (Genesis 4:10). It is clear from the cries that the rich have unjustly kept the wages. The withholding of fair wages is a problem that persists today; the disparity of power between the rich and the poor leads to abuse and exploitation.

Along with the withheld wages, the labourers themselves are crying out. They are harvesters, but they cannot keep what they harvest. They work for the landowner, who withholds fair

12 See my treatment of James 5:1–3 in '"The Refining of Your Faith"?', 199.

13 See Davids, *Epistle of James*, 177.

14 Allison, *James*, 672.

wages. The Old Testament law condemned the cheating of hired workers (Leviticus 19:13; see also Jeremiah 22:13). The cries of these workers likely remind the epistle's hearers of the cries of their ancestors while being oppressed in Egypt (Exodus 3:7). Like Israel in Egypt, the diaspora descendants have experienced injustice outside their ancestral homeland. The hearers of James may not all be labourers for local landowners, but they have faced marginalisation, discrimination, racism and injustice. As they cry out with their oppressed brothers and sisters, they receive this message from James.

The cries have not been in vain; they 'have reached the ears of the Lord Almighty'. The title here is Lord *sabaōth,* often translated as 'Lord of Hosts'. This title is used of God as the commander of the host of heaven. It is often associated with God pouring out wrath on the wicked (Psalm 59:5).[15] This instance in James has the most affinity with Isaiah 5, where the title is used four times (5:7, 9, 16, 24).[16] The oracle in Isaiah also condemns the rich for their unjust gain, luxurious living and depriving the poor of places to live (Isaiah 5:8–12).

James's description of the cries of the oppressed recalls Jesus's teaching after the parable of the persistent widow: 'Will not God bring about justice for his chosen ones, who cry out to him day and night? Will he keep putting them off?' (Luke 18:7).

Like the opening exhortation (1:2–4), this section of James serves as a theodicy, a defence of God's character in the face of evil. The disadvantaged hearers of James have been acquainted with injustice. They have been told not to usurp God's role as the judge (4:11–12). They are seeing the arrogance of those prospering around them (4:16; 5:5), but are called to humility. In their trials, they persevere and wait. Here, through James's feigned address to the rich, the audience hears an assurance

15 It also occurs in Romans 9:29, where it is an Old Testament quotation.

16 See Laws, *Epistle of James*, 202.

of God's just nature. Note James's use of the perfect tense: the cries 'have reached the ears' of the Lord. He is listening, and he knows about the injustice. Jesus continued, 'he will see that they get justice, and quickly' (Luke 18:8). The Lord Almighty, who is the only judge (James 4:12), will come with his armies and bring punishment on the oppressors (see Malachi 3:5).

The rich are doomed. James's disgraced diaspora hearers hear an eschatological assurance much like the prophet Zephaniah's:

> At that time I will deal
>   with all who oppressed you.
> I will rescue the lame;
>   I will gather the exiles.
> I will give them praise and honour
>   in every land where they have suffered shame.
> (Zephaniah 3:19)

Modern Christ-followers who face injustice can find consolation in James's message. They might experience systemic injustice, such as genocide or institutional racism. Or they could experience individual injustice, such as being enslaved or cheated by those in power. Either way, James's message to the wicked landowners assures them that God hears their cries. Their oppressors will be held accountable.

In James 5:5, the author gives more justification for the rich's guilt: they have indulged themselves in this life 'on earth'. This was how the rich man lived in the parable of the rich man and Lazarus (Luke 16:19), not caring for the poor man at his gate. Jesus declared woe on the rich because they have already been comforted in this life (Luke 6:24). The rich have fattened themselves, and the 'day of slaughter' is here. There is a bitter irony here, as they probably slaughter and consume animals for their feasts.[17] Like the rich fool described by Jesus, they feed themselves (Luke 12:19–20), unaware that the time has arrived for their slaughter. The end times are upon us, and the judge is 'at the door' (5:9).

James 5:6 contains a third accusation: 'You have condemned and murdered the innocent one.' The identity of the singular 'innocent one' is not explicit. The term can also be translated as 'righteous', as it is used in 5:16.[18] Some in early Christian tradition identify the 'righteous one' as Jesus himself,[19] and others propose that the victim is James himself. [20] However, the context indicates that this address is about landowners defrauding their workers. Besides, the letter is not written to Jerusalem – the place associated with Jesus's crucifixion and James's leadership – but to the diaspora (1:1). The best fit for this murder victim is a 'generic singular' for followers of God who are mistreated by the wealthy.[21]

How do the rich condemn and murder? First, the term 'condemn' refers to a courtroom. James has stated that the rich are dragging the disadvantaged into court (2:6). Condemnation of the rich living luxuriously and oppressing others is a repeated theme in biblical literature (such as 1 Kings 21:1–16; Proverbs 22:16; Amos 2:6; 5:11; Micah 3:1–3, 9–12).[22] Second, James states that the rich are killing those they condemn. Within the context, 'murdered' likely refers to the judicial system. The rich landowners oppress the farmers, leaving them with sparse wages

17 Davids, *Epistle of James*, 179.

18 The related terms 'condemned' (*katedikasate*) and 'innocent' (*dikaion*) create an ironic play on words.

19 Oecumenius, Bede and Cassiodorus. See Johnson, *Letter of James*, 304.

20 James's 'standard designation' was the 'Just'. See Martin, *James*, 182.

21 Blomberg and Kamell, *James*, 224–5. Also Moo, *The Letter of James*, 276. The NLT and CEV render this as 'innocent people'.

22 See the commentary at 4:2 regarding a possible allusion to the account of Naboth's vineyard.

or using the courts to take their land. Using their power, they could even be leveraging verdicts that imprison them, perhaps for life. In cultures characterised by patronage, including the Roman Empire, court verdicts were not determined by objective justice, but by influence and status. Also, to the Jewish hearers of James, denying someone their livelihood amounts to murder, as reflected in non-canonical wisdom literature: 'To take away a neighbour's living is to commit murder; to deprive an employee of wages is to shed blood' (Sirach 34:26–7).[23]

Ancient Chinese poet Tu Fu (eighth century), a government worker during the Tang Dynasty, seeing the wasted food in the emperor's palace and mourning his son's starvation, wrote about the disparity between the rich and poor:

> Behind vermillion gates wine and meats decay,
> On the road the bones of the frozen dead.[24]

Modern societies still display a growing gap between the rich and the poor. The rich have the influence and means to gain more, and they pass their wealth to the next generation. The poor must use all they have; it is difficult for them to generate more. Because wealth begets wealth, we see the rich becoming richer and the poor becoming poorer. In the midst of this, James's words continue to be relevant.

In his indictment against the rich in 5:1–6, James assures his hearers about God's just nature. The rich are living in luxury by exploiting the poor, but they will be held accountable in the end. The judge is near (5:8–9), and when worldly wealth fails,

---

23 Also see Wisdom of Solomon 2:6–20, where the 'ungodly' condemn the God-follower to death.

24 Eva Shan Chou, *Reconsidering Tu Fu: Literary Greatness and Cultural Context* (Cambridge: Cambridge University Press, 2006), 168. Cited in Cheung and Spurgeon, *James*, 98.

he will be the one to decide who is left standing and who will pass away.

The message addressed to the rich is a powerful encouragement to James's diaspora readers. Despite their shameful distance from the geographical centre of their faith, their disadvantaged status in their new homes and their rebellion against God (4:4), they can be 'innocent' (5:6). If they repent and humble themselves before God (4:9–10), they can have the esteem of being lifted up and being called friends of God (2:23).

II

# Persevere Patiently Until Judgment

## JAMES 5:7–11

After the two sections of apostrophe addressing outsiders for the sake of the audience, James gives a two-part ending to the epistle (5:7–11 and 5:12–20). James returns to addressing his hearers, with 'brothers and sisters' occurring five times in this two-part ending.

The first part of the ending, James 5:7–11, is a fitting way to end the main content of the epistle, as it (a) explicitly returns to the themes of the thesis statement and (b) gives a major exhortation following the content of the epistle.

James has a message of hope for his suffering hearers. He assures them of God's mercy and compassion. If they stick with their commitment to God, they will be ultimately rewarded.

*Patience in suffering*

**7** Be patient, then, brothers and
sisters, until the Lord's coming. See
how the farmer waits for the land
to yield its valuable crop, patiently
waiting for the autumn and spring
rains. **8** You too, be patient and stand
firm, because the Lord's coming is
near. **9** Don't grumble against one
another, brothers and sisters, or you
will be judged. The Judge is standing
at the door!

**10** Brothers and sisters, as an example of patience in the face of suffering,
take the prophets who spoke in the
name of the Lord. **11** As you know,
we count as blessed those who have
persevered. You have heard of Job's
perseverance and have seen what
the Lord finally brought about.
The Lord is full of compassion and
mercy.

The word 'then' connects this section to previous content – not just the material immediately preceding it, but the entire epistle. As discussed above, the letter contains repeated appeals to judgment. Every time people are judging, it is condemned (for example, 2:4, 6; 4:11–12), and every time God is the one judging, it is affirmed (for example, 2:12–13; 3:1; 4:12). The cumulative message becomes clear: people are not legitimate judges; only God is judge, and his righteous judgment will come in the end. The expectation of end-time judgment is the foundation for the exhortations of James: not showing favouritism, taming the tongue, showing good deeds as an expression of faith, having wisdom from above and being humble before God. This remains consistent with the epistle's thesis (1:12), which will be reprised in 5:11.

## *1. Patient until the end • James 5:7–10*

In James 5:7–11, the appeal to eschatological judgment is most explicit. Each saying in 5:7–9 points to the end times:

| Action | End-time expectation |
|---|---|
| Be patient . . .<br>The farmer waits for the rains | . . . the Lord's coming<br>valuable crop |
| Be patient and stand firm | . . . the Lord's coming is near |
| Do not grumble against one another | . . . or you will be judged<br>The judge is standing at the door! |

James begins in 5:7 with 'then', which connects to the previous material in the epistle. Again, the author has repeatedly discussed eschatological judgment in his exhortations to the hearers in 1:1–4:12. Also, the two sections of apostrophe (4:13–17 and 5:1–6), condemning two groups for their behaviour, are grounded in judgment. Now, in light of all of James's content about judgment, he gives a strong appeal to his hearers: be patient.

For James, patience is not merely a virtue. The hearers are to be patient 'until the Lord's coming'. The term for 'coming' is *parousia*, and in this context it refers to the second coming of Jesus. James has called Jesus 'the Lord' in 1:1 and 2:1, and 'the coming' of the Lord refers to the second coming of Christ elsewhere in the New Testament.[1]

In many cultures, the plight of the less fortunate leads to a certain fatalism. In South Asia, for example, those who are suffering will say, 'It is God's will,' as a coping mechanism to submit to their misfortunes.[2] However, James is not urging his hearers to despair, but to place their hope in the life to come. Their deliverance is coming.

James's use of the *parousia* in 5:7 is not to arouse fear. Unlike his scathing tone of 5:1–6, James urges his Jesus-following hearers to remember the coming of the Lord and place their hope in it. In all their suffering, they have hope. If they stay committed to Christ, they will experience God's mercy. The hearers are citizens of the kingdom, and they await the return of their king.[3]

In James 5:8, the audience hears that the *parousia* is near. This language of nearness is found in the sayings of Jesus, referring to the arrival of the kingdom of God and the last days.[4] With

---

1 See, for example, Matthew 24:27, 37, 39; 1 Corinthians 15:23; 1 Thessalonians 2:19; 2 Peter 1:16.

2 Brian Wintle, 'Matthew', in *South Asia Bible Commentary*, ed. Brian Wintle (Grand Rapids: Zondervan, 2015), 1234.

3 For a detailed treatment, see Robert J. Foster, *The Significance of Exemplars for the Interpretation of the Letter of James* (Tübingen: Mohr Siebeck, 2014), 146–7.

4 For example, Matthew 4:17; 24:33; Luke 10:11. See also Isaiah 46:13; 50:8; 51:5; 56:1.

the warnings that this life could be over unexpectedly (James 1:10–11; 4:14), James encourages the followers of Jesus that the end could come at any time.

Expecting the coming of the Lord, the hearers are to be patient. The hearers have many temptations around them: favouritism (see 2:1–4), selfishness (3:14; 4:2), anger and quarrels (1:19–20; 4:1–2) and unrighteous speech (3:9–10; 4:11). Giving in to these temptations leads to being enemies with God (4:4). As we approach the end of the epistle, the hearers receive the message that they must be patient rather than follow the path of sin, which leads to death (1:15).

James uses the image of a farmer who cannot control the autumn and spring rains but waits patiently. This is not a wealthy landowner (5:1–4), but one dependent on rain for his livelihood. Unlike the arrogant merchants and wicked rich, the small farmer acknowledges that God will provide (see Deuteronomy 11:14; Jeremiah 5:24–5).

Likewise, the hearers are exhorted to trust in the Lord and wait. The hope of a 'valuable crop' encourages the diaspora hearers that they will receive the eschatological blessing (see 1:12; 2:5). This contrasts the condemnation of the groups in the apostrophe sections of 4:13–5:6. Amid their trials, the hearers are encouraged to look towards the next life. Rather than placing their hope in worldly wealth now (like the rich do), they can expect good things when the end comes. This echoes Jesus's teaching that his persecuted followers are blessed (Matthew 5:10–12).[5]

Along with being patient, James's hearers are to 'stand firm'. The phrase here is woodenly 'establish your hearts'. While modern readers often consider the heart to be the seat of emotions, for James's hearers the 'heart' is the entire inner self.[6] The Old Testament idiom of 'strengthening the heart' refers to

5 James B. Adamson, *The Epistle of James* (Grand Rapids: Eerdmans, 1976), 192–3.

6 James is likely making a contrast with the rich who 'feed their hearts' in 5:5.

placing trust in the Lord (Psalm 111:8). As they expect the Lord's arrival, the hearers are called to strengthen their commitment to God.[7]

While he discusses the *parousia* in an encouraging light in 5:7–8, James still has a warning for his hearers: they must watch their behaviour. He calls them not to 'grumble against one another' in 5:9, lest they be judged. The command against complaining possibly recalls Israel in the wilderness (see Exodus 17:3; Numbers 11:1; 14:2). Again, James shows his concern for both speech and the harmony of the community. This patience, then, is exercised in relationships with others. Indeed, the prophets are an example of patience, since they suffered at the hands of other people. Amid their difficulties as both Jews and Christians, the hearers are to be patient, not lashing out against each other.

The motivation to refrain from grumbling is the expectation of judgment. With the warning, 'The judge is standing at the door!', James makes it clear that the coming of the Lord has two sides. While the faithful expect blessings, the Lord also comes as a judge. Indeed, if James still has the hard-working farmer from 5:7 in mind, the farmer does not have time or energy for disputes![8] For followers of Jesus, our behaviour reveals our priorities.

The phrase 'at the door' describes the imminence of the *parousia*. This phrase echoes the sayings of Jesus (Matthew 24:33; Mark 13:29).[9] The modern reader may object to James's message regarding the nearness of the second coming. After all, it has been two millennia, and Jesus has not returned. But the phrase 'at the door' does not necessarily denote that the return will happen soon. Rather, the coming of the Lord is ready to take place and could happen at any time. Instead of being like an

7 See the verb's usage in Acts 18:23; Romans 16:25; 1 Thessalonians 3:2.

8 Wiersbe, *Be Mature*, 163.

9 Christ's message for the church in Laodicea includes him standing at the door (Revelation 3:20).

aeroplane in the process of landing, the *parousia* is more like a helicopter hovering, with the ability both to be near and to land quickly. This is compatible with James's description of the ephemeral nature of life (4:14).

In James 5:10, the author exhorts his hearers to be patient with an example from the Old Testament. The prophets were faithful to God while being persecuted (see Matthew 5:12). In using the term 'example',[10] James designates the prophets as figures to imitate. James does not name particular prophets, but a natural fit would be Jeremiah,[11] who suffered greatly and is remembered as 'the weeping prophet'. Another example would be Daniel, who had an invading army destroy his home and force him to a faraway land. Despite his suffering, Daniel remained faithful.[12]

By invoking the example of the prophets, James places the hearers with honoured company. In the eyes of James's audience, the ones who 'spoke in the name of the Lord' are faith-heroes. Rather than react to their sufferings with despair or retaliation, the hearers of James can rejoice with patience, knowing that they, too, are servants of God.[13]

## *2. Persevere until the end • James 5:11*

Next, James shifts his focus to perseverance, which is related to patience. Since James designated the prophets to be an example of patience (5:10), 'those who have persevered' is not pointing back to the prophets, but pointing forward to the next example: Job. The different exemplars indicate the distinction between patience

---

10 See its usage in John 13:15.

11 Moo, *The Letter of James*, 288.

12 Sunukjian, *Invitation to James*, 109.

13 John Stott calls the mistreated prophets a 'noble succession'. See *The Message of the Sermon on the Mount*, Revised edition (Downers Grove: IVP Academic, 2020), 35.

and perseverance. On the one hand, the prophets suffered at the hands of other people. They embodied Jesus's ethic of non-retaliation, showing patience. On the other hand, Job suffered, not attack from others, but afflictions of poor health, poverty and bereavement allowed by God. Job's sufferings, albeit acute, are ordinary to humans.[14] Job, constantly entreating God for explanations for his sufferings, might not be seen as an example of patience.[15] But he did not follow the temptation to curse God (Job 2:9) and renounce his allegiance to him.[16] In his afflictions, Job displayed perseverance. James encourages his hearers that they would be included in good company.

For followers of Christ, our ability to persevere through suffering is directly tied to our view of the end times. Indeed, perseverance in faithfulness in light of the eschaton is a repeated New Testament encouragement (2 Timothy 2:12; Hebrews 10:36–9; 1 Peter 1:3–9; Revelation 2:3) If we neglect the coming of the Lord, we often react to our difficulties in ways that are displeasing to God, like grumbling, vengeance and selfishness. However, if we place our hope in the *parousia*, we can more readily weather the storms.

James refers to the ones who persevered as those 'we count as blessed'.[17] This statement of blessing reprises the thesis statement of the epistle: 'Blessed is the one who perseveres under trial' (James 1:12). As discussed above, this is the closing of the grand *inclusio*.

With the return to the thesis statement, James signals that the letter is ending. There is a noticeable topic shift in the next

---

14 Laws, *Epistle of James*, 215.

15 Some suspect that James refers to the noncanonical Testament of Job, where Job is commended for his perseverance and encourages his children to 'be patient'. See Foster, *Exemplars*, 134.

16 Foster, *Exemplars*, 156–8.

17 There may be a play on words, or an instance of catchwords, between 'patience' (*makrothymia*) and 'bless' (*makarizō*).

saying; we will see that James 5:12 fits best with the closing section. Therefore, this saying in 5:11 – blessing for those who persevere – wraps up the main content of the epistle.

The statement of blessing and the example of Job is a fitting ending. The hearers are facing trials: marginalisation, exploitation and oppression. These trials come with temptations that they must resist: favouritism, having faith with no deeds, selfishness, envy and slander. James reminds his hearers of his main idea: that those who endure in adherence to God will be approved in the end.

The motivation for perseverance in James 5:11 is 'what the Lord finally brought about'. In quick succession, James appeals to what his hearers have known, heard and seen: the account of Job. What the Lord finally brought about in Job's situation was the restoration of his possessions and family. His suffering was not the 'end',[18] and we observe that the Lord is 'full of compassion and mercy'.

For the hearers of James, the 'end' is not their current trials, but what God brings about at the *parousia*. After the stern warning of eschatological condemnation to the rich in 5:1–6, James turns back to the hearers and assures them that if they persevere, they will receive God's compassion and mercy. Like Job, they must not turn their backs on God amid their difficulties.

Again, James reminds his hearers that their perseverance in loyalty to God, expressed in behaviour such as caring for the poor and singly beneficial use of the tongue, will result in eternal reward. This has been described earlier as the 'crown of life' (1:12) and the inheritance of the kingdom (2:5). The faithful

18 The term here is *telos*, which can be rendered as 'end' or 'goal'. See James's use of the cognate adjective in 1:4 and 1:25. Some consider this phrase in James 5:11 to refer to God's intended purpose, while others interpret it as the result that the Lord produces. Ultimately, they are not mutually exclusive. For a detailed discussion, see Luke L. Cheung, *The Genre, Composition and Hermeneutics of James* (Carlisle: Paternoster, 2003), 251–2.

Christ-followers, while facing marginalisation and oppression in the diaspora, must not rely on the things of this world (see 1:11; 4:14). They must place their hope in the coming of the Lord. Those who persevere will be judged favourably and receive heavenly reward.

As followers of Christ, we might never understand why we suffer. Our difficulties can look like they will never end. But we have hope – the end could come at any time. God is merciful, and he will reward those who are faithful to him.

# 12

# Final Exhortations

## JAMES 5:12–20

After returning to the thesis statement in James 5:11, the rest of the epistle (5:12–20) makes up some final exhortations for the hearers. Since 5:7–11 is an appropriate ending to James's letter, creating a grand *inclusio*, these final sayings serve as an epilogue or a postscript. Fittingly, these sayings have elements that display consistency with other Greek letter endings.[1]

First, the phrase 'above all' (5:12) is a common element in ancient Greek letters, also occurring in 1 Peter 4:8. Second, James discusses oaths in 5:12, which are featured at the end of Greek letters. Third, James contains content about health in 5:14–15, consistent with a health wish found in other Greek letters, notably 3 John 2. Fourth, James writes about prayer in 5:13–18, with Greek letters offering an ending prayer or a request for prayer, including 2 Corinthians 13:7; Ephesians 6:18–20; 1 Thessalonians 5:25, Hebrews 13:18. While we will see that James departs in novel ways from these conventions, these elements show that the epistle 'is dictated by the epistolary form' as Davids says.[2]

Since these elements share the adherence to letter-ending convention, the modern teacher or preacher of James can treat 5:12–20 as one teaching unit, while distinguishing between the subunits as follows.

---

1 See my detailed treatment in *Eschatological Approval*, 44–5, 178–81.

2 Davids, *Epistle of James*, 181.

12 Above all, my brothers and sisters,
do not swear – not by heaven or by
earth or by anything else. All you
need to say is a simple 'Yes' or 'No'.
Otherwise you will be condemned.

*The prayer of faith*

13 Is anyone among you in trouble?
Let them pray. Is anyone happy?
Let them sing songs of praise. 14 Is
anyone among you ill? Let them call
the elders of the church to pray over
them and anoint them with oil in the
name of the Lord. 15 And the prayer
offered in faith will make the sick
person well; the Lord will raise them
up. If they have sinned, they will be
forgiven. 16 Therefore confess your
sins to each other and pray for each
other so that you may be healed.
The prayer of a righteous person is
powerful and effective.

17 Elijah was a human being, even
as we are. He prayed earnestly that
it would not rain, and it did not rain
on the land for three and a half years.
18 Again he prayed, and the heavens
gave rain, and the earth produced
its crops.

19 My brothers and sisters, if one of
you should wander from the truth and
someone should bring that person
back, 20 remember this: whoever
turns a sinner from the error of their
way will save them from death and
cover over a multitude of sins.

## *1. No need for oaths • James 5:12*

As stated above, the topic shifts between James 5:11 and 5:12. This saying about oaths is consistent with the convention of Greek letter endings. However, rather than offering an oath, James follows the convention in a novel way, with a prohibition of swearing.

The phrase 'above all' is a curious one here. After all, James has addressed much more grave issues, like murder and adultery. Surely oaths are not worse than these! However, 'above all' is a common element in Greek letter closings and signals some final content that may differ from the letter's main thrust.

To be sure, James has already discussed the misuse of speech (1:26; 3:1–12; 4:11–12). Here, James's prohibition is consistent with his concern that his hearers would use the tongue righteously. Also, like the other exhortations in James, the motivation is grounded in judgment: 'Otherwise you will be condemned'.[3]

James's prohibition of oaths is similar to Leviticus 19:12, which teaches that false swearing profanes God's name.[4] Likewise, Deuteronomy 23:21–2 warns that the people should be quick to fulfil a vow, lest they be guilty of sin. But if they refrain from the vow completely, they will not be guilty. This is the key to the prohibition of oaths – one incurs condemnation if they do not keep it.

The most notable parallel with James 5:12 is, once again, found in the Sermon on the Mount (Matthew 5:33–7). Jesus, recognising that the Torah urged his followers to keep their oaths, commanded his disciples not to make oaths at all. As we will discuss more below, Jesus calls them to a different standard of truthfulness.

In teaching about swearing 'by heaven' and 'by earth', James (and Jesus) addresses a common abuse of oaths during his time. Some believed that swearing by something like their right hand – a common object far removed from God – would make it harmless to deceive or inadvertently break their oaths. Others took oaths more seriously, but they were afraid of using God's name lest they violate the commandment not to misuse it (Exodus 20:7). Instead, they would swear using surrogate objects such as heaven, Jerusalem or God's throne.[5] A popular belief went like this: the further removed the object was from God's name, the less harm there was in breaking the oath.

---

3 The word phrase for 'condemned' features the noun *krisis*, or 'judgment'. It is used twice in James 2:13. The verb form is found in 2:12; 4:11–12; 5:9.

4 Its proximity to the love command in Leviticus 19:18, which James calls the 'royal law' (2:8), suggests that James's ethics have a foundation in Leviticus 19. See Johnson, 'Leviticus 19 in James'.

5 This practice is called *kinnuyim*. See Craig S. Keener, *A Commentary on the Gospel of Matthew* (Grand Rapids: Eerdmans, 1999), 194.

The belief that there are grades, or levels, of truth persists today. I remember children in the playgrounds attempting to assure others by saying, 'I swear,' and then raising their oath to a higher level with, 'Cross my heart and hope to die, stick a needle in my eye.' George Washington started the tradition of a new American president taking an oath with a hand on the Bible, as if his word itself was not good enough. Others might swear 'on a stack of Bibles' – rather than one – as if their statement would be more reliable. These practices betray the belief of a greater punishment for deception if the oath invokes things closer to God or grave consequences. One imagines that God somehow pays closer attention when someone makes an oath mentioning him or something sacred.

But the reality is that God hears every word we speak, whether in a public court of law or in a private interaction with another person. We are accountable to him for our words. James calls his hearers not to have levels of truth, because God is a witness to everything. He calls for one standard: tell the truth all the time. Keep your word all the time. This is what it means to have 'a simple "Yes" or "No"'. James calls his hearers to integrity. If we deceive, defraud, or break our word, this leads to condemnation when judgment comes.

Ultimately, if we take James's teaching to mean not taking an oath in a court of law, we miss his point. James is declaring that Christ-followers should never need oaths. The very existence of swearing reveals the true problem: people are continually deceiving each other. We call others to utter extra words, sign their name or do a hand motion for us to trust one another.

A mark of the Christ-follower should be truthfulness and reliability. Oaths should not take the place of integrity. While they are tempted by the ways of the world, the hearers of James are set apart as Christians. Bearing the name of Christ to the world, they can show God's intent for society by keeping their promises.

God hears every word we speak, and he will hold us accountable in the end. As we live in expectation of judgment, let us hold one standard of truth: 'Yes' or 'No'.

## *2. Exhortations to prayer • James 5:13–15*

In James 5:13–18, our author gives several exhortations, linked together by the concept of prayer, or human communication with God. Instead of an actual prayer found in many Greek letter endings of the time, James gives content about prayer. This matches the historical accounts about James. Eusebius described James as a man of constant prayer, making his knees like those of a camel.[6]

As we will see below, it is best to disassociate James 5:16 – the statement about praying for one another resulting in healing – from the exhortations in 5:13–15.[7] We will discuss James 5:13–15 and 5:16–18 as distinct subsections within the final exhortations of James.

James's exhortations in 5:13–15 are addressed to the communities of his hearers, indicated by the phrase 'among you'.[8] These sayings contain three parallel constructions, each featuring a condition with a corresponding exhortation. The NIV renders these conditions as questions:

| **Verse** | **Condition** | **Exhortation** |
|---|---|---|
| 13a | Is anyone among you in trouble? | Let them pray. |

6 *Ecclesiastical History*, 2.23. Eusebius of Caesarea, *Ecclesiastical History, Books 1–5*, 129.

7 See my treatment of this section in Daniel K. Eng, 'Healing from Sin: The Effective Prayer in Jas 5:16', *Trinity Journal* 44, no. 1 (2023): 38–41.

8 See 3:13 and 4:1 and note its absence in 4:13–5:6.

| 13b | Is anyone happy? | Let them sing songs of praise. |
|---|---|---|
| 14 | Is anyone among you ill? | Let them call the elders of the church . . . |

In the first condition, someone 'in trouble' is suffering misfortune. James does not specify what sort of trouble this might be, but this term is not commonly used for illness.[9] In his opening exhortation, James has already addressed 'trials of many kinds' (1:2). As we have discussed above, the diaspora hearers of James are minorities – both ethnic and religious – and suffer marginalisation, low social status and exploitation (2:6). James may have in mind their 'trouble' in the courts or being cheated (5:4). The prayer in the exhortation could be an entreaty for God to remove misfortune in the present life, just like Jesus and Paul prayed (Matthew 26:39, 42; 2 Corinthians 12:8).[10] It could also be a prayer for justice against one's oppressors, as Jesus teaches with the parable of the persistent widow (Luke 18:7–8). A prayer for justice would fit with James's repeated emphasis on end-time judgment (see 5:1–6, 9, 12). A third possibility for this prayer would be a request for fortitude and wisdom to endure the suffering (see 1:2–5, 12; 5:11).

Ultimately, just like he does not name a particular sort of 'trouble', James does not specify a particular sort of prayer. These requests are fitting responses to suffering misfortune, and one can pray for all of them: deliverance, justice and fortitude. The point James makes, as he continues in 5:13–15, is that his hearers should be in prayer.

9 Nystrom, *James*, 304.

10 Followers of Jesus with unfulfilled requests find company with Jesus himself, who prayed for the 'cup' of his suffering to be taken away, but submitted to the Father's will.

The second condition in James 5:13 is 'happy'. Unlike the 'trouble' in the first condition, James is not describing an external circumstance, but an emotion.[11] Another rendering can be 'cheerful'. While the two conditions are not opposites, there is a contrast between them: feeling bad or feeling well.

The exhortation for the happy person is like the first: direct communication to God. In this case, the happy person is to 'sing songs of praise'. This is not revelry for its own sake but praise directed towards the Lord. The verb *psallō* – see the root for 'psalm' – in biblical literature refers to 'singing to the Lord'.[12] With 'among you' addressed to the church (5:14) in this context, there is probably a corporate element in this singing.[13]

With the contrast of the two conditions of 5:13, James teaches that God should be addressed in all situations: times of difficulty as well as times of rejoicing. Prayers of thanksgiving, lament, petition and praise are always given to the Lord. This is consistent with Paul's exhortation to 'pray continually' and 'give thanks in all circumstances' (1 Thessalonians 5:17–18).

The third condition (James 5:14–15) involves a person who is 'ill'.[14] Instead of a wish for good health found in many Greek letter endings, James gives a variation of this convention with an instruction about health.

In this command, James describes an illness that makes someone bedridden. Calling the elders to come, having them pray (in contrast to 5:13, where the troubled or happy person prays), and the elders being 'over' the sick person points to the sick person being helpless and bedridden.

---

11 Moo, *The Letter of James*, 299. The verb occurs in Acts 27:22 and 25.

12 Johnson, *Letter of James*, 329–30. See its usage in Judges 5:3; Psalm 7:17.

13 The New Testament instances of *psallō* occur largely in the context of community. See 1 Corinthians 14:15; Ephesians 5:19.

14 Paul uses the verb to refer to spiritual weakness (for example, Romans 4:19), but it is used for physical illness almost everywhere else in the New Testament. See Blomberg and Kamell, *James*, 242.

Indeed, in this exhortation, the 'elders' are the main actors. They are likely the leaders of the church, and the verb for 'call' has an official tone to it. The early church had appointed elders to formal offices (see Titus 1:5; 1 Timothy 5:17). James referred earlier to a synagogue as the place of meeting (see the comments at 2:2), but this term for 'church' refers to a gathered group of believers in the New Testament.[15]

Coming to the sick person, they must 'pray over them'. In addition to praying, the elders must 'anoint them with oil in the name of the Lord'. The oil might have medicinal value, as seen in the parable of the good Samaritan (Luke 10:34). Mark 6:13 is a close parallel, with the Twelve anointing the ill with oil and healing them.

Three points about the oil must be made here. First, the anointing is a subordinate action to the primary command for the elders, which is to pray. This is supported by the grammar as well as James 5:15, which mentions only the prayer. Second, the intention of this practice is distinct from the Roman Catholic sacrament of extreme unction, or last rites. Here in James, the prayer and anointing are not for spiritual purification before death, but for physical healing.[16] Third, prayer and oil do not have power on their own. The actions must be done 'in the name of the Lord', indicating submission to God's will (see 4:15).[17] The person would not be healed by the acts of prayer or anointing, but by God.

James 5:15 states that the sick person will become well. While the verb used can refer to eternal salvation,[18] the context with

---

15 Johnson, *Letter of James*, 330. The word for church, *ekklēsia*, is the root of the term 'ecclesiology'.

16 See the discussion in Blomberg and Kamell, *James*, 242–3.

17 George M. Stulac, *James* (Downers Grove: IVP Academic, 2011), 182.

18 James uses *sōzō*, which is also found in 1:21; 2:14; 4:12; 5:20. It is largely used to convey any kind of preserving, or saving from harm. See its usage for physical salvation in Matthew 14:30 and 27:40. See 'Σῴζω', in BDAG. Notably,

'ill' and 'sick', indicates that it refers to physical healing.[19] The NIV's 'raise up', then, refers to the person getting out of bed after recovering from the illness.

The teacher or preacher of James should note two points that pertain to modern application. First, James's teaching is an encouragement to someone reluctant to ask boldly from the Lord. God hears the prayers of his people, and he is compassionate and powerful. Second, such prayers are to be done in the community. Rather than merely praying alone, the sick person is called to have the church leaders pray over him or her.

Some modern readers might be concerned about the statement in James 5:16, having encountered or heard about so-called 'faith healers' who have deceived or defrauded people. Others might object to James's statement, having prayed for a sick person, only to be devastated when their loved ones do not recover. Such scenarios require sufficient pastoral care.

We must acknowledge a qualification for this prayer. James designates the elders' prayer as a 'prayer offered in faith'. This phrase recalls the prayer for wisdom in 1:5–6. It raises questions: when a sick person does not recover, is it the fault of those praying? Do they simply not have enough faith, as the 'faith healers' might state? While space does not allow for a discussion of the relationship between our prayers and God's sovereignty,[20] the phrase 'prayer offered in faith' offers clarification. The appeal to 'faith' recognises its object: a powerful God who alone decides whether to have the sick recover. Just like the earlier qualification of 'in the name of the Lord', this prayer 'offered in faith' is an act of submission to God's will. After all, God does not always restore a sick person. The apostle Paul experienced his

---

spiritual salvation is never the result of intercessory prayer in the New Testament.

19 See my treatment in Eng, 'Healing from Sin', 44–9.

20 An accessible resource is W. Bingham Hunter, *The God Who Hears* (Downers Grove: InterVarsity Press, 1986).

own prayer for physical recovery as unanswered (2 Corinthians 12:7–9). He submitted to God, who had a good purpose for the suffering.

Ultimately, then, a prayer for healing is not an incantation that is only effective if activated in a particular way. Neither is it an appeal to a detached deity who behaves in unpredictable, capricious ways. Christ-followers will do well to recognise that God's will is supreme, and that he is compassionate. Our bold prayers acknowledge God's power while expressing submission to his good will.[21]

To be sure, the hypothetical scenario of the bedridden person can also have a spiritual element. The final part of James 5:15 discusses the possibility of the sick person's sin. Some might cite this 'sin' to support the idea James is using 'well' and 'raise them up' in the spiritual sense. But the 'sin' here is not definite; it is made contingent by the word 'if'. The definite element is clearly the person's physical ailment. Sickness does not always occur as a direct result of sin, as the innocence of Job (see 5:11) indicates.[22]

The contingency still indicates a possibility that the person's sickness indeed results from sin. After all, there are instances of such a connection in the New Testament (Mark 2:1–12; 1 Corinthians 11:29–30). James therefore urges the sick person to address any possible spiritual causes of the illness. As 1 John 1:9 reminds us, God will forgive us for our sins if we confess them.

In the three hypothetical scenarios in 5:13–15, James exhorts his hearers towards prayer. Whether in trouble, in rejoicing or in illness, Christ-followers are to communicate with God.

---

21 For a discussion on the nuances of this saying, see Blomberg and Kamell, *James*, 243–5.

22 Also see John 9:2–3.

## *3. Prayer for sin • James 5:16–18*

James 5:16 is best seen as more closely tied to the following sayings rather than the ones preceding it.[23] James signals a new line of thought by departing from the question–resolution format to a direct exhortation. Also, rather than giving exhortations for single persons in particular scenarios ('Is anyone . . .?'), James now returns to addressing the hearers of the epistle as a group.

This subsection of the final exhortations focuses particularly on prayers for sin. Continuing the theme of prayer, the word 'therefore' ties this command in 5:16 with the previous discussion on prayer, going back to 5:13. Since prayer is encouraged in all the scenarios in 5:13–15 for single persons, the hearers should definitely pray in mutual confession of sins.

One might be tempted to think that the 'healing' in 5:16 is physical. This is understandable; 5:16 shares the common elements 'sin' and 'prayer' with the saying about the sick person in 5:15. The fact that the sick man recovers and is raised appears to suggest that the hearers of James in 5:16 would also be physically healed.

But James 5:16 departs from 5:15 in significant ways, pointing to a shift in topic. First, James's penchant for using catchwords – perhaps to aid the memory – opens the possibility that 5:15 and 5:16 are disparate.[24] Second, James's general exhortation to 'confess your sins' does not derive from the scenario about the bedridden person; sin is only a contingency in 5:15. Note that the first scenario, mentioning someone's 'trouble', could also

23 I give a detailed argument for the disassociation of 5:16 from 5:14–15 in Eng, 'Healing from Sin', 38–41.

24 For example, there is a shift in topic from 'trial' to 'temptation' through the same term in both 1:12 and 1:13. See the commentary regarding 'The cohesiveness of James 1', in chapter 1, and 1:12–13.

include the possibility of sin. Third, while the command in 5:15 is to have the elders pray, the command in 5:16 is mutual: 'pray for each other'.[25] Fourth, the resolutions also differ: while the sick man is 'raised' from his physical ailment, 5:16 only mentions 'that you may be healed'. There is no indication that there is a physical ailment that all the hearers share. Fifth, the term for 'heal' here, when it is associated with sins and lawlessness in the Old Testament, refers to God's mercy and forgiveness on the people.[26] Most notably, 1 Peter 2:24, citing Isaiah 53:5, uses this term to refer to the 'healing' for followers of Christ because of the cross.

Exhorting his hearers to mutual confession and prayer, James again shows his concern for the community. For example, he has discussed showing mercy (2:13), taming the tongue (3:2–12), peacemaking (3:17–18) and not grumbling against one another (5:8). Here, with two instances of 'each other', he is concerned about how the community's sins have impacted each other.

Sin is not merely a 'vertical' problem, as if it only impacts an individual's relationship with God. Sin is also a 'horizontal' problem, impacting relationships within the community. The phrase 'that you may be healed' is plural, suggesting that James is considering the 'fights and quarrels' (4:1–3). Their relationships are fractured because of sin. While confessing sins to God leads to forgiveness (see 1 John 1:9), confessing sins to one another, with mutual prayer, urges God to heal the group. James, then, is writing about healing the effects of sin in the community.

What will lead to the community being healed? First, James prescribes mutual confession of sins. Public confession is a repeated practice for Israel (Numbers 5:7; Proverbs 28:13; Daniel 9:5–6). Second, James prescribes mutual prayer. Like the

---

25 So also Laws, *Epistle of James*, 232.

26 See the usage of *iaomai* in 2 Chronicles 7:14, 30:20; Psalm 41:4 (40:5 LXX); Isaiah 6:10; 53:5.

psalmist in Psalm 41:4, the hearers' prayers for one another should acknowledge their sins and ask for healing.

Note that James is calling his hearers to confess their sins to 'each other'. There is no mention of an authoritative figure, like a priest, to whom to confess. The activity of confession and prayer is mutual.

In the statement about the prayer of a righteous person, the context indicates that those who confess their sins are the righteous ones. They are the ones who have humbled themselves before the Lord (4:10) and receive forgiveness, thereby becoming 'righteous'. Encouraging his hearers to pray for one another, James gives his hearers confidence that prayers for healing – in the context of mutual confession of sins – are powerful and effective.

The example of Elijah in James 5:17–18 is strong evidence that the 'powerful and effective' prayer in 5:16 refers not to prayer in general, but to a particular sort of prayer. After all, if James meant 5:16 to refer to prayer in general, the choice of Elijah is a curious one. One can more readily think of other figures known for their prayers, such as David, Daniel or even Job. Why choose Elijah? For that matter, why choose Elijah's prayer for rain? One can readily think of other, more dramatic instances of Elijah praying, like raising the widow's son or calling fire from heaven at Mount Carmel.

However, when read in the particular context of a prayer for the community's *healing from the result of sin*, Elijah's example fits very well. James appeals to Elijah's prayer in regard to sin in order to encourage his hearers to pray for healing from sin as well. Elijah prayed for the rain to stop (1 Kings 17:1), because of the people's sin, their apostasy led by Ahab. After the people turned back from their sin to recognise God, Elijah prayed and the rains came (1 Kings 18:39–45).

This account of prayer for *healing from sin* relates to Solomon's prayer of dedication earlier in 1 Kings, which foresees a time of no rain because of the people's sin (1 Kings 8:35–6). His prayer echoes the warnings from Moses that their idolatry will lead to no rain (Deuteronomy 11:16–17; 28:24). Solomon's prayer declares that the people will pray and confess their sin, and the Lord will hear from heaven and forgive them. The reprise of Solomon's dedication is found in 2 Chronicles, after which the Lord responds:

> When I shut up the heavens so that there is no rain, or command locusts to devour the land or send a plague among my people, if my people, who are called by my name, will humble themselves and pray and seek my face and turn from their wicked ways, then I will hear from heaven, and I will forgive their sin and will heal their land. (2 Chronicles 7:13–14)

If, as the scholarly consensus states, 1–2 Chronicles is written to post-exilic returnees to the land,[27] it contains the message that God forgives and heals the land in response to repentance. Centuries later, James urges his hearers to confess their sins in prayer, with the appeal to Elijah's prayer for healing of the land. The diaspora hearers are encouraged that they, too, can pray for their sins and receive healing together. Despite their distance from the land that is a crucial part of their identity, they are not cut off from God (see 4:8). The cross of Christ facilitates that they can be forgiven and healed (see 1 Peter 2:24).

From what will the community be healed? Corporate healing probably addresses relational conflict, as James has already discussed the dissension and conflict in their communities (4:1–3) and the godly wisdom that results in peace-making (3:17–18). Indeed, for modern faith communities, the humble posture of mutual confession and prayer can lead to reconciliation – healing of relationships.

To be sure, the 'healing' in James 5:16 does not preclude physical healing. After all, the people's sin in 1 Kings (and 2 Chronicles)

---

27 Eugene Merrill, *A Commentary on 1 & 2 Chronicles* (Grand Rapids: Kregel, 2015), 22–3.

resulted in drought, locusts and pestilence. Paul indicates that a community's sin can result in physical ailments (1 Corinthians 11:30). Perhaps there are physical conditions that have resulted from the sin of the community. But, unlike the scenario with the sick man in 5:15, it is definite that this healing in 5:16 remedies the result of sin.

Taken out of context, the saying about a 'righteous person' could be taken to refer to a special class of Christ-followers, as if only certain ones can have powerful and effective prayers. But James is not putting Elijah in a different class from his hearers. On the contrary, he writes that Elijah 'was a human being, even as we are'. His appeal to Elijah's ordinary nature encourages the hearers that they, too, can engage in effective prayer. In the context, what makes someone righteous is confession of sins, which submits to God's ways (see 1 John 1:9). Thus, they can be counted as righteous people, and their prayers, like Elijah's, will be powerful and effective.

Likewise, the modern teacher and preacher of James can encourage Christ-followers to confess their sins in community and pray for their healing. Is there unresolved conflict, jealousy or slandering? How might the relationships in the community be negatively impacted by sin? Could the consequences even include physical conditions? Healing can start with the confession of sins.

## *4. Restoring a wanderer • James 5:19–20*

With the final exhortation, James addresses a brother or sister wandering from the truth. He reminds his hearers of the good that comes from restoring this wanderer. In doing so, he exhorts them back to his main concerns in this letter: urging his hearers to repent (see 4:4–10).[28]

28 Moo, *The Letter of James*, 316.

The 'truth' here is not merely the doctrine of the Christian message. What counts is not merely assenting to declarations (see James 2:19), but doing what God's word says (1:22–4). The concept of wandering, or being led astray, is consistent with the biblical imagery portraying obedience as walking (for example, Deuteronomy 8:6; 2 John 6). One who wanders from the truth is 'a sinner' in the way of error (see James 5:20).

In what ways could a brother or sister wander from the path of righteousness? They could be deceived by others, as Jesus warns (Matthew 24:5). They could be led by their own desires (James 1:14). Perhaps they have become firmly entrenched in the world as enemies of God (4:4).

With 'one of you', James identifies the wanderer as someone who is part of the Christian community. However, what truly matters is whether they have the sort of faith that saves, and this is demonstrated in their behaviour (2:14–17). The action to 'bring that person back' restores them, both to the faith and to the Christian community.

To bring someone back involves approaching them about their sin. Jesus commanded that his followers must point out the fault of a brother or sister to win them over (Matthew 18:15). The apostle Paul, too, commanded that those in the church should restore a person caught in sin (Galatians 6:1).

But is restoring a sinner compatible with James's condemnation of judging someone else (4:12)? After all, Jesus commanded, 'Do not judge' (Matthew 7:1). But James gives us guidance to help relieve this tension. First, the 'sinner' is wandering from the 'truth'. The truth is a standard that is outside us, determined by the only Lawgiver. This is the standard to which both the wanderer and the restorer must adhere; we will all face the judge (4:12). James does not condemn the person who upholds God's law. Rather, James condemns speaking against the law and judging it (4:11), elevating our human standard above God's standard. Judging the law usurps God's role as the lawgiver and creates human standards.

Second, restoring a wanderer 'will save them from death' (5:20). This pointing out of their sin, then, is done out of concern. James's teaching recalls the Lord's charge to the prophet to warn someone that their wicked ways will lead to death (Ezekiel 3:18–21; 33:7–9). The intent is to save them, not to elevate oneself and speak against the law (James 4:11). Jesus explains his command of 'Do not judge' by stating that the same standard will be applied to the one judging. He warns against hypocritical judgment (Matthew 7:2–5). This confrontation in James 5:19 is not a hypocritical sort of judging, but one done out of love. The restorer is concerned that the wanderer will not walk on the path to death.

Pointing out the sin of someone else is always fraught with risk. The person being confronted may even respond in anger to the person doing the correction. These angry responses often come because of the perception that the corrector is judging them.

But restoring a wanderer is not standing and facing them as the judge. The posture is akin to standing side by side with someone, pointing to the standard of the true Judge that we must all face. This is 'turning' a sinner; the goal is to point them back to the right path. As Paul states, this must be done gently, and with the restorer watching themselves, lest they also be tempted (Galatians 6:1).

For the twelve tribes of the diaspora (1:1), the call to restoration resonates deeply. Whether by choice or by force, the hearers are outside their ancestral land. Scattered among the nations, they recall their ancestors' Exile, which resulted from their wandering from the truth. Here in James, the stakes are eternal, as seen in the thesis statement of 1:12. Wandering from the truth will result in an even direr consequence.

James clarifies the motivation for his command to restore a brother or sister. First, it will save them from death. This is not merely physical death, since a sinner would still physically die. This 'death', then, is the result of sin, as James has declared (1:15) and is attested elsewhere in the New Testament (John 3:14–16; 1 Corinthians 15:21–2, 54–7). Physical death will precede a reckoning for either eternal blessing or eternal suffering (Matthew 25:31–46). With end-time judgment in view, James urges his hearers to watch out for one another, lest they wander onto the path that leads to eternal death.

To be sure, 'save' here in 5:20 probably communicates that the restorer is only *facilitating* salvation from eternal death. After all, James declares that only one can save (4:12). God is the enactor of salvation, with the restorer serving as the agent used by God.[29]

Second, restoring a sinner will 'cover over a multitude of sins'. The text does not specify if covering refers to preventing the sin or making the sin invisible. Either way, the result is the same: there is no penalty. The consequences of sin are suppressed (Nehemiah 4:5; Psalm 32:1; 85:2; 1 Peter 4:8).[30] This is well paired with saving the wanderer from eternal death.

In writing this epistle, James's motivation is divine judgment. He urges his hearers to persevere in faithfulness and stand the test (1:12). With many temptations around them, the diaspora Christ-followers are compelled to seek the best interests of their brothers and sisters. For communities of Christ-followers of any age, we must keep one another on the right path as we await the crown of life.

---

29 See also George Hart and Helen Hart, *A Semantic and Structural Analysis of James* (Dallas: SIL International, 2001), 164.

30 Some hold the view that the sins being covered are those of the restorer. See Dibelius, *James*, 258–9; Laws, *Epistle of James*, 240–41. But 5:13–18 contains a pattern that the subject benefits another, and the result of the actions in 5:19–20 benefit the wanderer. See my argument in *Eschatological Approval*, 183–4.